A READER'S DIGEST SONGBOOK

THE EASY WAY TO PLAY

100 Favorite Songs of Faith, Friendship & Love

Editor: William L. Simon
Music arranged and edited by Dan Fox
Senior Staff Editor: Mary Kelleher
Art Director: Judy Speicher
Staff Editor: Richard Hessney
Electronic Publishing Specialist: Mark Pengelski
Illustrations by Judy Speicher and Nancy Stahl
Annotations by Clair W. Van Ausdall
Music Associate: Elizabeth Mead
Rights Manager: Lisa Garrett Smith

READER'S DIGEST GENERAL BOOKS
Editor-in-Chief, Books and Home Entertainment: Barbara J. Morgan
Editor, U.S. General Books: Susan Wernert Lewis
Editorial Director: Jane Polley
Art Director: Evelyn Bauer
Research Director: Laurel A. Gilbride
Affinity Directors: Will Bradbury, Jim Dwyer, Joseph Gonzalez, Kaari Ward
Design Directors: Perri DeFino, Robert M. Grant, Joel Musler
Business Manager: Vidya Tejwani
Copy Chief: Edward W. Atkinson
Picture Editor: Marion Bodine
Head Librarian: Jo Manning

THE READER'S DIGEST ASSOCIATION, INC.
Pleasantville, New York/Montreal

ISBN 0-89577-833-5

THE EASY WAY TO PLAY
100 Favorite Songs of Faith, Friendship and Love

Index to the Sections

Index to the Songs

INTRODUCTION

Faith . . . friendship . . . love. . . . Old-fashioned concepts, to be sure, but nothing more reassuring or more energizing has ever captured the essence of the unique heartland spirituality that imbues our American lifestyle. Faith . . . friendship . . . love. . . . Old-fashioned concepts—and how we like to sing about them!

Here are 100 of everybody's favorite melodies, everybody's favorite lyrics dealing with those very ideals, drawn from many walks of life, full of that almost inexpressible joy and gratitude that can be best satisfied by playing and singing—directly from the heart. Here in this collection you'll find 100 familiar but ever-new expressions of the intimacy of togetherness, personal visions of the truth, unsought gifts of healing or comfort, identifications with hope for all the world . . . each one promising that love is better than sadness, that trust is more life-affirming than despair, and that beauty is just a smile away.

These are songs for everyone, culled from everywhere. They represent the house of worship, whichever and wherever it may be for you. In equal variety they represent the Broadway stage, the Sunday school class, the Hit Parade and the patriotic parade, the revival meeting, the choir loft and the movie palace. They exemplify the rich and the poor, the proud and the humble, the fortunate and the struggling. Again and again in these songs,

as we turn each page, we can find ourselves anew, often at our best, sometimes at our neediest.

Lifting our voices in song is one of the ways that for generation upon generation we have shown ourselves at our best. And when we sing about faith and friendship and love, particularly, we are making a heaven of the earth we live on and love in. Welcome to those Elysian Fields, that melodic paradise!

How This Book Helps You to Play Real Music

The Easy Way to Play 100 Favorite Songs of Faith, Friendship & Love has been designed primarily for two groups of people: those who have limited piano skills and those who play the electronic keyboard, either proficiently or as a beginner. If you play another instrument, you can use the book too, as you'll see when you read on. Whatever the instrument, everything is designed to let you play the melodies you know and love with the very least effort and with the utmost comfort and convenience. All have been arranged for your playing pleasure by the masterful Dan Fox, who has arranged every Reader's Digest music book—all 17 of them.

Now take a look at the explanatory sample bars of "I Believe" printed below, then read on and discover just how this book can work for you.

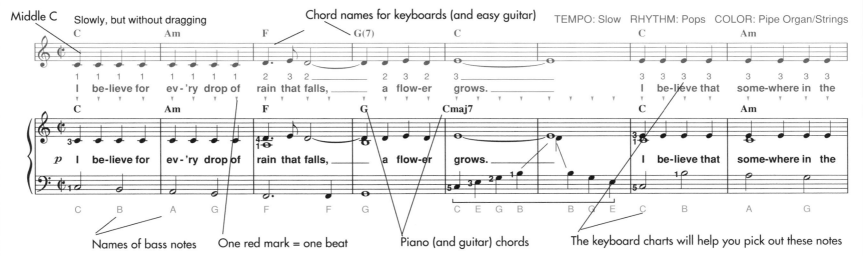

The blue staves and lyrics are for keyboard players. The black systems are for easy piano and more experienced keyboardists.

Middle C — Slowly, but without dragging — Chord names for keyboards (and easy guitar) — TEMPO: Slow   RHYTHM: Pops   COLOR: Pipe Organ/Strings

Names of bass notes — One red mark = one beat — Piano (and guitar) chords — The keyboard charts will help you pick out these notes

For Electronic Keyboard Players

Anything printed in blue is designed especially for you. This includes the top line of the music—the treble, or right-hand, clef—with the notes numbered for those who can't read music, as well as the lyrics and the suggested tempos, rhythms and colors. Of course, if you can play the piano and use your electronic keyboard with both hands, just as you do an acoustic piano keyboard, it's advisable to play the fully scored piano arrangements for bass and treble clefs, printed in black. See the section on "For Easy Piano Playing," which follows, for further information.

For chords to accompany the melody, look to the letters, also printed in blue, above the keyboard line. (The simplest, inexpensive monophonic [one-note-at-a-time] keyboards will not play chords.) For this and other instructions, please consult the manual that came with your instrument. The notes that can sound automatic chords will probably be identified on the backboard behind the keys of your instrument. But to help you find them, you can use one of the keyboard charts with letter names that are provided with this book. (See "About the Keyboard Charts" on the following page.)

You don't have to know what notes constitute each chord; just press the indicated key with your left hand. For a simple major chord you usually press one key or button. For example, to play a C chord, press a C in the designated bass portion of the keyboard, below Middle C. That key will automatically play the three notes of a C chord (C, E and G). If you want a D chord (D-F#-A), just press a D. To play minor chords or major and minor 7th chords (indicated in the music by such notations as Cm, G(7), Gm(7) and so on), you may have to press two, three or four fingers of your left hand. Different makes of keyboards require different techniques. For example, on a Casio, to play a minor chord, such as Cm, you play the C plus any neighboring note directly above the C. On a Yamaha, you would play the C plus any note below the C. If your instrument does not play 7th chords, you can still get a satisfactory harmony with the basic chord—say, a G rather than a G(7). In fact, the parentheses around the 7 indicate that the 7th chord is optional. Again, consult your manual.

At the top right-hand corner of the first page of each song, we have

3

suggested tempos, rhythms and instrumental colors for that tune. Always remember that our suggestions are just that—suggestions. As you become more familiar with the keyboard, you'll begin to experiment with the music, and you'll have fun choosing your own instrumental sounds and different rhythms for a song.

Counting time. If you know how the song goes, you will probably know how long each note should be held—even if you don't know a half-note from a quarter-note. We don't go into musical notation here. However, we do show you where the beats are by the red marks underneath the lyrics; each mark (▼) is to be counted as one beat. Your electronic keyboard probably has a tempo light that blinks on each beat, so you can coordinate with that—one ▼ for each blink.

Automatic rhythms. The rhythms you can use on a song depend on the make and model of your instrument. Some electronic keyboards can play a polka rhythm; others cannot. Some have a "cha-cha" button, others a "bossa nova." Some can combine two rhythms to sound like a rhythm they don't have on a single button. Again, study your manufacturer's manual. And experiment.

Instrumental colors. Most keyboards offer piano, flute, guitar, strings, organ and a few other instrumental sounds, or colors. Some of the more versatile models allow you to mix different colors, which may enable you to come closer to the actual instrument sounds or even to create your own sounds. Once again, consult your manual, since different makes offer different choices.

Once you know your keyboard and its many possibilities, you may be able to simulate an orchestral arrangement even if you are not a trained musician. Certainly your satisfaction will come easier and faster than you ever dared to dream, and you'll have great fun getting there. And remember, players of electronic instruments have a great advantage: you can play with earphones, and no one has to hear what you're doing until you're ready to turn on the speaker and dazzle them.

For Easy Piano Playing
Perhaps you're a piano student, or a retiree who is "getting back" to the piano after not touching it for most of your adult years. Or you're a wind instrument player who has always wanted to "play a little piano." Then our very easy two-hand arrangements, printed in black, are for you. (Remember, the top line and lyrics, printed in blue, are for electronic keyboards.)

Since some players may have little experience with the bass, or left-hand, clef, our arrangements usually don't ask you to play more than a single note at a time with your left hand. The name of each bass note is printed in red under the lines, under each note. Until you grow more familiar with the bass notes, you can use the keyboard chart to identify the notes in the two octaves from Middle C down. You might also find the beat marks (▼), printed in red, helpful.

More experienced players can refer to the chords that we've indicated at the top of the piano lines in black. These chords are sometimes different from those on the blue lines, substituting more complex harmonies that are not in the automatic chord bank of electronic keyboards.

For Non-Keyboard Players
If you play a single-note instrument, such as a violin, flute, saxophone, clarinet, oboe, trumpet, harmonica or melodica, you can play from the electronic keyboard melody line (printed in blue), reading the notes. However, if you want to play in combination with another instrument, you would have to be sure that the other instrument is pitched in the same key. Clarinet, trumpet and tenor or soprano saxophone, for example, are B-flat instruments and can play together from the same music. Piano, guitar, accordion, autoharp, violin, flute, oboe and some recorders are in C. Alto and baritone saxophone and mellophone are in E flat, and so on.

If you play accordion or autoharp, you can certainly play from the blue lines. But depending on the options your particular instrument provides, you might get more variety out of the harmonies in the piano staves, printed in black.

For Guitarists
Guitarists can begin with the simpler chords indicated in the blue lines and then graduate to the more advanced chords shown above the black treble clefs. We've provided guitar diagrams for all of the chords used in our arrangements; they can be found at the back of the lyric booklet that accompanies this songbook.

Now all that's left is for you to sit down and start playing. Go back to the index, select one of your favorites and enjoy!

Yours in faith, friendship and love,
The Editors

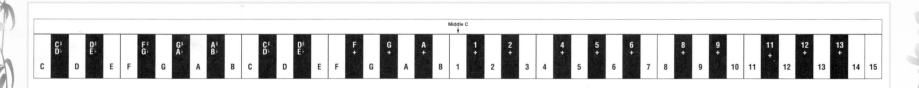

About the Keyboard Charts
With this book we've provided the keyboard chart shown above in three different sizes—for pianos, full-size keyboards and most mid-size keyboards. The appropriate chart may be set up behind the keys of your piano or keyboard and will help you identify the notes as they are used in this book.

The numbered notes on the chart are for use primarily by electronic keyboard players who can't read music. If you are in this category, you will be playing the top line of the music, printed in blue. These are the treble, or right-hand, notes.

The lettered notes are the two octaves of notes in the bass, or left-hand, clef—to the left of Middle C—on both electronic keyboards and pianos.

To position the chart on your instrument, first find Middle C, which will be Number 1. It is in the center, or just to the left of center, of the keyboard, the first white key below the grouping of two black keys.

Then the black key directly up from C, or C sharp (C#) (which is the same as D flat (D♭), becomes 1+. D becomes 2. D sharp (D#), the same as E flat (E♭), becomes 2+, and so on, following the diagram.

Notes in the bass clef are identified by their letter names rather than by numbers. Position them as shown on the diagram. Starting on the C two octaves below Middle C, the white keys will read C-D-E-F-G-A-B and repeat again up to 1 (Middle C). The black keys will read C#/D♭, D#/E♭, F#/G♭, G#/A♭, A#/B♭, until you reach the F#/G♭, G#/A♭ and A#/B♭ just to the left of Middle C. The chart will identify these as F+, G+ and A+. The reason for this is that the melody sometimes reaches down to those keys below Middle C, and, for non-music-readers, this is consistent with the 1+, 2+ identifications of the melody from Middle C upward.

Climb Ev'ry Mountain (page 16)

Richard Rodgers and Oscar Hammerstein II's *The Sound of Music*, based on the life of the singing Trapp family of Austria, swept Broadway off its feet in 1959. Lyricist Hammerstein, though already suffering with the cancer that would kill him not long after the show's opening, poured his own courage into one of the most inspirational songs in the score, advice sung by the Abbess to the young aspiring nun Maria. Hammerstein added his own penciled note in the margin of the music: "Until you find the life you were meant to lead, you are not living."

Count Your Blessings Instead of Sheep (page 8)

Irving Berlin, always an insomniac, had spent a number of sleepless weeks in 1954. His wife, Ellin, finally proffered him some advice: "Count your blessings instead of sheep." Whether or not it helped him nod off that particular evening we don't know, but it did obviously inspire him to write this Christopher Award–winning song. It was first sung by vocalist Eddie Fisher at a dinner honoring the 300th anniversary of Jewish emigrés to this country and, at Berlin's request, was dedicated on that occasion to "our greatest blessing, President Dwight Eisenhower." "Count Your Blessings" also became part of the score for the film *White Christmas* that same year, along with "Blue Skies" and the title song.

I Believe (page 20)

Singer Jane Froman starred in a television show called *USA Canteen* that aired in 1952 during the Korean War. A serviceman's letter inquiring about her beliefs touched her deeply, and she asked the show's songwriting team to compose something that would speak to anyone whose faith was wavering. Ervin Drake, one of the songwriters, said they tried to encapsulate a message of hope "for the common man." Just how eager the country must have been for such reassurance became evident when Froman's glowing performance set off a chain of recordings by other singers that culminated in Frankie Laine's million-seller. "I Believe" also won the Christopher Award for that year's finest inspirational song.

I'd Like to Teach the World to Sing (in Perfect Harmony) (page 10)

First heard as a Coca-Cola commercial in 1971 with the lyric "I'd like to buy the world a Coke," this tune (and the ad) caught the public's attention immediately. The Hillside Singers, eight singers in the original ad, changed the lyrics to "I'd like to teach the world to sing" and recorded the song. In England, meanwhile, the popular '60s group The Seekers reorganized themselves as The New Seekers and recorded it too, scoring a kind of sequel to their first million-seller, "Look What They've Done to My Song, Ma." It became the U.K.'s 1971 Song of the Year and a hit in the U.S. as well.

The Impossible Dream (page 22)

Based on Miguel de Cervantes' 1605 Spanish novel *Don Quixote, Man of La Mancha* lit up the Broadway stage in 1966 for more than 2,000 performances and furnished star Richard Kiley with the biggest song of his career, "The Impossible Dream." Both the show and the song were based on the philosophy of Cervantes' 20th-century fellow countryman Miguel de Unamuno: "Only he who attempts the absurd may achieve the impossible." The show's original-cast recording remained a best-seller for more than three years, and its most popular excerpt, "The Impossible Dream," has been recorded nearly 200 times. Surprisingly, the musical was composer Mitch Leigh's first appearance on Broadway.

Look for the Silver Lining (page 18)

In 1920, Broadway producer Florenz Ziegfeld ordered a special song for his special new star's upcoming revue, *Sally*. The star was none other than dazzling Marilyn Miller, and the song was "Look for the Silver Lining," which Jerome Kern and Buddy De Sylva had written a season earlier for a production that never found its way to the stage. *Sally* proved a prodigious hit for Miller, who, playing a bedraggled young dishwasher, offered this uplifting message. It became so closely identified with her that it was used as the title for her film biography in 1949.

May the Good Lord Bless and Keep You (page 26)

Actress Tallulah Bankhead, whose mahogany voice was a favorite of the '50s, headlined the Sunday evening radio program *The Big Show*. Her music director, Meredith Willson, seeking inspiration for a closing song, remembered his mother's weekly benediction to the Sunday school class she had taught for years in Mason City, Iowa: "May the good Lord bless you and keep you." Hurriedly he dashed off a setting of that phrase—it took him less than 24 hours—and taught it to Bankhead in time for that week's broadcast. The song was a smash and has remained so ever since.

The Sound of Music (page 13)

Who could forget the sight of peasant-skirted Julie Andrews whirling joyously in the flower-dotted Austrian Alps to the accompaniment of "The Sound of Music" in the film version of the great 1959 Broadway musical that starred Mary Martin? Both Andrews and Martin shone in the pivotal role of Maria—governess, music teacher and eventually wife and stepmother of a real-life clan that became famous worldwide as the Trapp Family Singers. Rodgers and Hammerstein proved their hunch to be right when they maintained that, in the face of certain critics who found the show oversweet, American audiences would never tire of "happiness and honest sentiment."

You'll Never Walk Alone (page 6)

The American composer Cole Porter, known for the witty sophistication of his own songs, once said that the best songs of Richard Rodgers and Oscar Hammerstein II had "a kind of holiness" about them. Certainly "You'll Never Walk Alone," from their 1945 musical *Carousel*, could be characterized thus, or as "an anthem to hope," in the words of another fan. *Carousel* was based on a play by Hungarian dramatist Ferenc Molnár, who paid Rodgers and Hammerstein the compliment of preferring their upbeat ending— in which Julie's love for Billy the carnival barker gloriously conquers death— to his own more somber one.

from *Carousel*   Words by Oscar Hammerstein II; Music by Richard Rodgers

TEMPO: Slow   RHYTHM: March/Country/Swing   COLOR: Strings

Count Your Blessings

from *White Christmas*   Words and Music by Irving Berlin

TEMPO: Slow   RHYTHM: Swing   COLOR: Flute, Sax, Synth Reed or Strings

I'd Like to Teach the World to Sing
(in Perfect Harmony)

Words and Music by B. Backer, B. Davis, R. Cook and R. Greenaway

TEMPO: Moderate   RHYTHM: Big Band/Swing   COLOR: Reeds or Brass

* Repeat the measures between the 𝄋 and the final ending.

12

THE SOUND OF MUSIC

from *The Sound of Music*   Words by Oscar Hammerstein II; Music by Richard Rodgers

TEMPO: Moderate   RHYTHM: Salsa or Pops   COLOR: Strings, Chorus

13

Climb Ev'ry Mountain

from *The Sound of Music*
Words by Oscar Hammerstein II;
Music by Richard Rodgers

TEMPO: Moderate   RHYTHM: Pops   COLOR: Strings, Organ or Flute

LOOK FOR THE SILVER LINING

from *Sally* Words by Buddy De Sylva; Music by Jerome Kern

TEMPO: Moderate RHYTHM: Big Band/Swing COLOR: Violin

I BELIEVE

Words and Music by Ervin Drake, Irvin Graham, Jimmy Shirl and Al Stillman

TEMPO: Slow   RHYTHM: Pops   COLOR: Pipe Organ/Strings

The Impossible Dream

from *Man of La Mancha*　　　Words by Joe Darion; Music by Mitch Leigh

TEMPO: Moderate　RHYTHM: Slow Rock　COLOR: Strings/or Vox Humana/Oboe/Horns

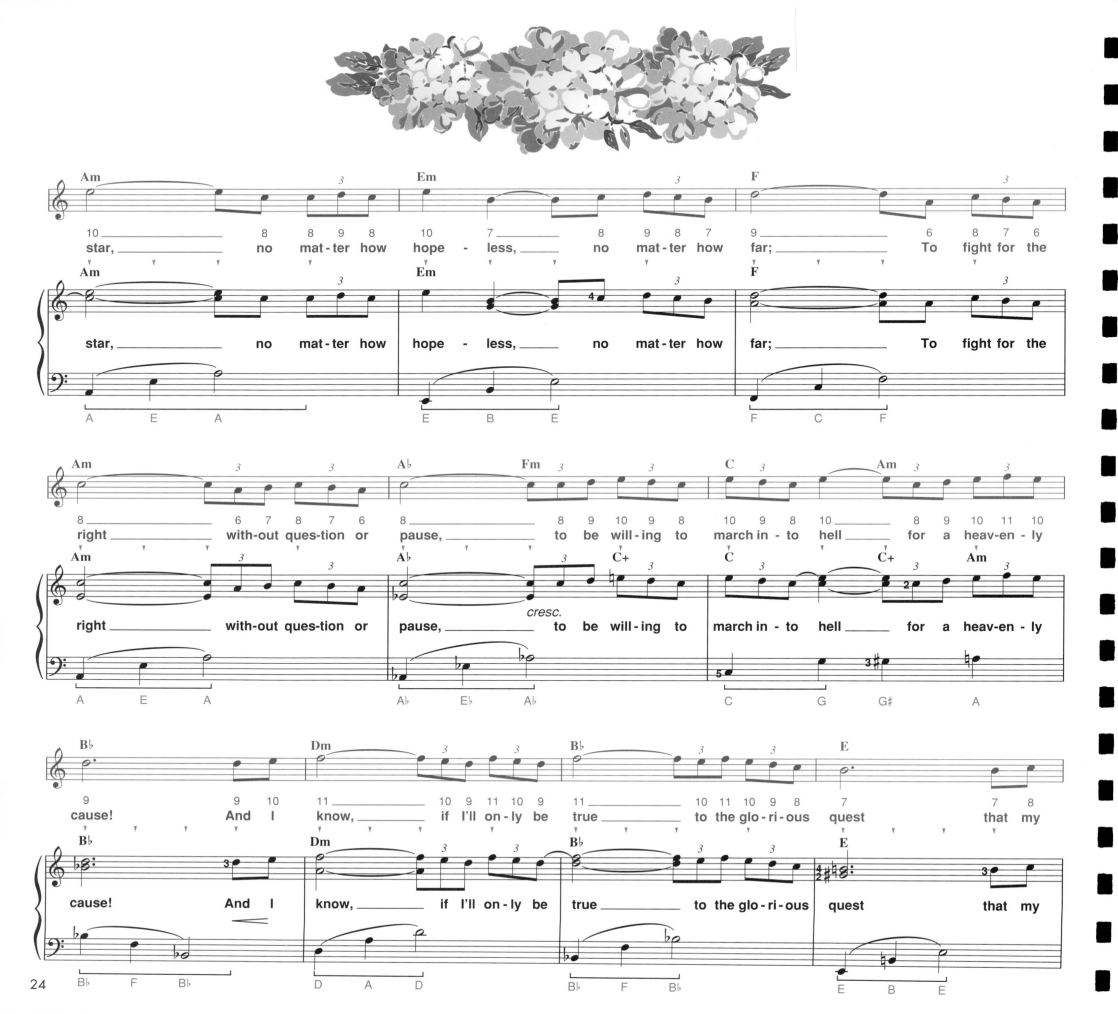

May the Good Lord Bless and Keep You

Words and Music by Meredith Willson

TEMPO: Moderate   RHYTHM: Slow Rock   COLOR: Flute and Harp

Dear Hearts and Gentle People (page 32)

When America's balladeer Stephen Foster died on a New York City street in 1864, bitterly alone and poverty-stricken, having squandered both his talent and his little remaining money on drink, he was discovered to have in his tattered overcoat pocket three pennies, a dollar or two in scrip and a half-sheet of paper on which he had scrawled the phrase "dear hearts and gentle people." Perhaps it was the beginning of another lovely ballad (such as "My Old Kentucky Home," completed only a few days before). In any case, its fragile poetic charm seemed to cry out for a song setting, and some 85 years later, in 1949, Bob Hilliard and Academy Award winner Sammy Fain recognized that need by completing a lyric and adding an equally moving tune.

One God (page 29)

Florence Mary Fitch's book *One God*, published in 1944, was written principally to clarify for young people the presence of God in whatever religion they had been brought up in, whether Roman Catholic, Protestant or Jewish, and to remind them that, while the details of forms of worship might vary, the God each of them worshipped was the same. The daughter of a Congregational minister, Fitch had been born "at the sound of the church bell," as her father never wearied of telling her, and taught philosophy and religion at Oberlin College. Dave Kapp, then head of Decca Records, asked songwriters Ervin Drake and Jimmy Shirl, who had already had a success with "I Believe" (page 20) on a similar subject, to compose something using the title of Professor Fitch's book, and they came up with their hymn-like "One God" in 1954.

Put a Little Love in Your Heart (page 34)

Jackie DeShannon won national fame as a singer when she opened for The Beatles during their triumphant first American tour in 1964. She was also an admirer of Bob Dylan and recorded his "Don't Think Twice, It's All Right" and "Blowin' in the Wind." But singing is only one of her talents; she also paints, sculpts, acts and writes songs, often with another composer's help. Her "Put a Little Love in Your Heart," with its light gospel beat, demonstrates the last talent. She recorded it in 1969, and in the summer of that year watched it romp to the top of the pop charts.

That's What Friends Are For (page 42)

Carole Bayer Sager and Burt Bacharach wrote "That's What Friends Are For" in 1982 for the movie *Night Shift*. The film was a great success, and the song achieved its own life, first in 1985 when Rod Stewart recorded it and especially a year later when Dionne Warwick, whose unique sensitivity to the subtlety of Bacharach songs continues to this day, had a No. 1 hit singing with such "friends" as Elton John, Gladys Knight and Stevie Wonder. "That's What Friends Are For" was voted Song of the Year for 1986, and, by prior design, all the proceeds were donated to AIDS research. Bayer Sager and Bacharach have not only had spectacular separate careers in music but, as a married couple, a dual one too.

What the World Needs Now Is Love (page 39)

"Most songwriters," says lyricist Hal David in a book about his work with composer Burt Bacharach, "like to think they know when they have written a hit. A few years ago Burt and I thought we liked a song we'd written, but then decided we were wrong and put it away." Several years later they got it out again because they were short one song for a recording session, and they decided it wasn't bad at all. Jackie DeShannon, herself the writer of many wonderful songs in this same inspirational mode, had the biggest hit with "What the World Needs Now Is Love," in 1965, and was followed by Dionne Warwick, whose chemistry with Bacharach and David has resulted in a string of spectacular successes.

You Light Up My Life (page 36)

In 1977, Joe Brooks's song "You Light Up My Life" won both an Oscar for its use in the film of the same name (also written, directed and produced by the multitalented composer) and a Grammy—despite the fact that nearly every major music publisher and record company had turned it down, and even Brooks had let it languish on his "rejects" pile. His own career had been a long time coming, though he played almost every known musical instrument and had attended five colleges, albeit without the customary reward of a degree. Still, he continued to write jingles in Hollywood until this film, his first, finally put him in the limelight. Debbie Boone's recording further helped rescue the song and its composer from obscurity; it was a big hit for her—top-place chart honors for 10 weeks—and she sang it at the Academy Award ceremonies the year it won.

You've Got a Friend (page 44)

Carole King, who was born in New York City but influenced chiefly by rock and country singers like Bill Haley, Elvis Presley and Fats Domino, wrote "You've Got a Friend" for her award-winning 1971 *Tapestry* LP, which captured a Grammy as Album of the Year and has sold 15 million copies over the years. King won two additional Grammys for Best Female Pop Vocal and Song of the Year for "You've Got a Friend," though James Taylor's recording was more successful commercially than hers, leaping to the top of the charts also in 1971.

One God

Words and Music by Ervin M. Drake and Jimmy Shirl

TEMPO: Slow   RHYTHM: Slow Rock II   COLOR: Clarinet/Synth Reed, Organ or Strings

31

Dear Hearts and Gentle People

Words by Bob Hilliard; Music by Sammy Fain

Put a Little Love in Your Heart

Words and Music by Jimmy Holiday, Randy Myers and Jackie DeShannon
TEMPO: Slow   RHYTHM: Rock   COLOR: Rock or Jazz Organ, Jazz Guitar

Slow rock and roll

1. Think of your fel - low man, lend him a help - ing hand, put a lit-tle love_ in your heart. _____ (1) _
2. An - oth - er day _ goes by, and still the chil - dren cry, put a lit-tle love_ in your heart. _____ (2) If
3. Take a good look _ a - round, and if you're look - in' down, (3) _

You see, it's get - ting late, oh, please don't hes - i - tate, put a lit-tle love_ in your heart. _____ And the world _
you want the world _ to know we won't let ha - tred grow,
I hope when you _ de - cide kind-ness will be _ your guide,

YOU LIGHT UP MY LIFE

Words and Music by
Joseph Brooks

36

What the World Needs Now Is Love

Words by Hal David; Music by Burt Bacharach

TEMPO: Moderate   RHYTHM: (Jazz) Waltz   COLOR: Jazz Organ

That's What Friends Are For

Words and Music by Carole Bayer Sager and Burt Bacharach

TEMPO: Slow   RHYTHM: Rock   COLOR: Electric piano

YOU'VE GOT A FRIEND

Words and Music by
Carole King

TEMPO: Moderate   RHYTHM: Pop   COLOR: Rock or Jazz Organ

*Repeat the chorus to the ⊕ , then skip to the Coda

Everything Is Beautiful (page 52)

Ray Stevens, who got into the music business as a disc jockey at the age of 15, broke out of that mold in the early '60s when he began writing and recording a series of hilarious take-offs and novelties, among them "Ahab the Arab," "Harry the Hairy Ape," "Gitarzan" and "The Streak." Then, in 1970, came "Everything Is Beautiful," an abrupt change of pace that introduced his listeners to a new ease and sincerity in his songs. Stevens also achieved a new success, with his own TV show and a new momentum to his performing career. Of course, he was back in his usual mode a few months later, with "Bridget the Midget" and "America, Communicate with Me." Many singers have recorded "Everything Is Beautiful," among them Tennessee Ernie Ford and Jim Nabors.

Happy Trails (page 55)

After Roy Rogers' first wife died, leaving him with three children, he married the leading lady of his many Western films, Dale Evans, thus establishing one of the most enduring husband-and-wife partnerships in show business. Not only did they act and make stage appearances together, but Dale Evans wrote such songs as "Happy Trails" expressly for their radio and TV show of the '50s. Since then, she said, "We have used 'Happy Trails' in every one of our public appearances together." With an ambling gait and laid-back lyrics, the song suggests all the warmth and contentment of perfect days in companionable cowboy country.

I Believe in Music (page 58)

"My daddy started me off singing in the church choir as soon as I could hold up the hymnal," says Mac Davis, who, though he still does not read or notate music, plays the guitar and had his own rock 'n' roll band in college. When a major record producer met him at a Nashville party and heard him sing, Davis was encouraged to start recording, and thus began his highly successful string of hits, many of them his own songs. "Stop and Smell the Roses" dates from the early '70s, as does "I Believe in Music." A number of other singers have also achieved hit recordings with Davis songs, including Andy Williams, Kenny Rogers, Lou Rawls and Glen Campbell.

It Is No Secret (What God Can Do) (page 56)

Born in Texas, Stuart Hamblen spent a number of years in California singing cowboy songs, and writing for and acting in Westerns, usually as one of the "bad guys." He also wrestled with a severe drinking problem. After he had conquered it, an actor friend asked Hamblen how he had managed to do it. He replied, "God helped me, and He'll help anybody who'll let Him. It is no secret what God can do." Later that evening, his own words kept flitting around in his head, and a melody began to take shape. In 17 minutes the song was finished—words *and* music. That was in 1951, and "It Is No Secret" is now one of the top-ranking gospel songs everywhere.

One Day at a Time (page 68)

Actor-songwriter Kris Kristofferson, a former Rhodes Scholar at Oxford University whose special interest was the poetry of William Blake, made his own kind of musical poetry in 1974 when he wrote the country classic "One Day at a Time," with Marijohn Wilkins supplying the lyrics. The first hit recording was by Marilyn Sellars, and Don Gibson also had a big seller. In 1980, though, Cristy Lane pushed "One Day at a Time" to No. 1 on the country charts—her biggest hit ever.

(There'll Be) Peace in the Valley (for Me) (page 60)

Thomas A. Dorsey was raised by a Baptist minister father and church organist mother in Chicago, where he established his own band, accompanied Ma Rainey and wrote blues songs, including "Tight Like That." Then, in 1932, he gave up the blues and devoted himself to gospel music. As he put it, "I had a dream one night that God took me by the hand, and He said 'Do it!' So I *did* it!" He certainly did. In his long career he wrote some of the most deeply felt and beloved gospel songs: "Take My Hand, Precious Lord" (page 144), "A Little Talk with Jesus," "If You See My Savior" and "Peace in the Valley," the last a big country hit for Red Foley in 1951. Revered as the father of gospel music, Dorsey died in 1993 at the age of 93.

Shall We Gather at the River? (page 62)

Robert Lowry was pastor of a prominent Baptist church in Brooklyn when he wrote "Shall We Gather at the River?" This was his recollection: "One afternoon in July of 1864, the heat was oppressive, and I lay exhausted, resting. Visions of the future passed before me. Brightest of these visions were the throne, the heavenly river and the gathering of the saints. I began to wonder why hymnists had written so much about the river of Death and so little about the pure water of Life. As I mused, the words began to construct themselves, first as Christian inquiry and then as an answer to Christian faith. The music came with the words."

What a Difference You've Made in My Life (page 64)

At least two singers owe a good deal of their early success to Nashville writer Archie Jordan's upbeat love song "What a Difference You've Made in My Life," composed in 1977. Ronnie Milsap's mellow version made it to the top of the best-seller charts that year and won him a Country Music Association Award. Amy Grant, who consciously avoids any songs that are "too preachy" or, as she puts it, "life-changing," had a gospel hit two years later that crossed over to receive considerable air play on country and pop radio stations.

Wings of a Dove (page 49)

The dove has for centuries been a familiar symbolic figure in religion. It was a dove that returned to Noah's Ark with the olive branch that signaled the end of the Flood and God's making peace with humankind. When Jesus was baptized by John the Baptist, God caused a dove, embodying the Holy Spirit, to descend upon His Son. And Renaissance artists painted the dove as a symbol of peace. The composer of "Wings of a Dove," Bob Ferguson, a bird-and-wildlife photographer, filmmaker and record producer, says he wrote the song as "a personal expression of faith and joy in achieving a goal" (the goal being the completion of 13 films on wildlife). Ferlin Husky scored a big success with his 1960 recording of the tune.

Wings of a Dove

Words and Music by Bob Ferguson

TEMPO: Fast   RHYTHM: Waltz   COLOR: Organ or Synth Reed

49

Additional Verses

2. When Noah had drifted on the flood many days,
He searched for land in various ways.
Troubles, he had some, but wasn't forgotten;
He sent him His love on the wings of a dove.
(Repeat Chorus)

3. When Jesus went down to the waters that day,
He was baptized in the usual way.
When it was done, God blessed His Son;
He sent Him His love on the wings of a dove.
(Repeat Chorus)

EVERYTHING IS BEAUTIFUL

Words and Music by Ray Stevens

TEMPO: Moderate   RHYTHM: Big Band/Swing, Slow Rock I   COLOR: Clarinet/Flute

52

* Repeat the measures from the 𝄋 to the word "Fine."

Additional Verse

We shouldn't care about the length of his hair
  or the color of his skin.
Don't worry about what shows from without
  but the love that lives within.
We gonna get it all together now,
  and ev'rything gonna work out fine.
Just take a little time to look on the good side, my friend,
And straighten it out in your mind.
And ev'rything is beautiful *etc.*

HAPPY TRAILS

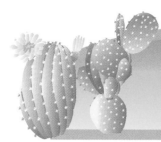 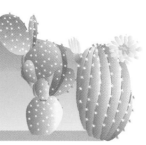

Words and Music by Dale Evans

TEMPO: Slow   RHYTHM: Big Band, Swing, Slow Rock I   COLOR: Harmonica/Oboe

55

It Is No Secret
(What God Can Do)

Words and Music by Stuart Hamblen

TEMPO: Moderate   RHYTHM: Country, Big Band/Swing   COLOR: Organ, Jazz Guitar

1. The chimes of time ring out the news; An - oth - er day is through. Some - one slipped and fell. Was that some-one you? You may have longed for add - ed strength, your cour - age to re - new. Do not be dis - heart - ened, for I have news for you:

2. There is no night, for out in His light, you'll nev - er walk a - lone. Al - ways feel at home where - ev - er you may roam. There is no pow'r can con - quer you while God is on your side. Just take Him at His prom - ise. Don't run a - way and hide:

I Believe in Music

Words and Music by Mac Davis

Moderately, with a lilt

TEMPO: Moderate RHYTHM: Country, Slow Rock I COLOR: Piano, Oboe

Well, I could just sit a-round mak-in' mu-sic all day long; Long as I'm mak-in' mu-sic, I know I can't do no-bod-y wrong. And who knows, may-be some-day I'll come up with a song that makes peo-ple wan-na stop their

Chorus

fuss-in' and fight-in' just long e-nough to sing a - long.____ Ev-'ry-bod-y sing: I

fuss-in' and fight-in' just long e-nough to sing a - long.____ Ev-'ry-bod-y sing: I

be-lieve in mu - sic, __ I_____ be-lieve in love._____

be-lieve in mu - sic, ____ I_____ be-lieve in love._____

Additional Verses

2. Music is love, love is music, if you know what I mean.
   People who believe in music are the happiest people I ever seen.
   So clap your hands, stomp your feet, shake your tambourine,
   Lift your voices to the sky, God loves you when you sing.
   Everybody sing: *(Repeat Chorus)*

3. Music is the universal language, and love is the key
   To brotherhood and peace and understanding, to livin' in harmony.
   So take your brother by the hand and sing along with me,
   And find out what it really means to be young and rich and free.
   Everybody sing: *(Repeat Chorus)*

(There'll Be) Peace in the Valley (for Me)

Words and Music by the Rev. Thomas A. Dorsey

TEMPO: Moderate   RHYTHM: Waltz or None   Color: Strings or Organ

60

SHALL WE GATHER AT THE RIVER?

Words and Music by
the Rev. Robert Lowry

TEMPO: Moderately slow   RHYTHM: Country or None*   COLOR: Reed Organ or Harpsichord

*Play each chord where its symbol appears. A "/" means to repeat the previous chord.

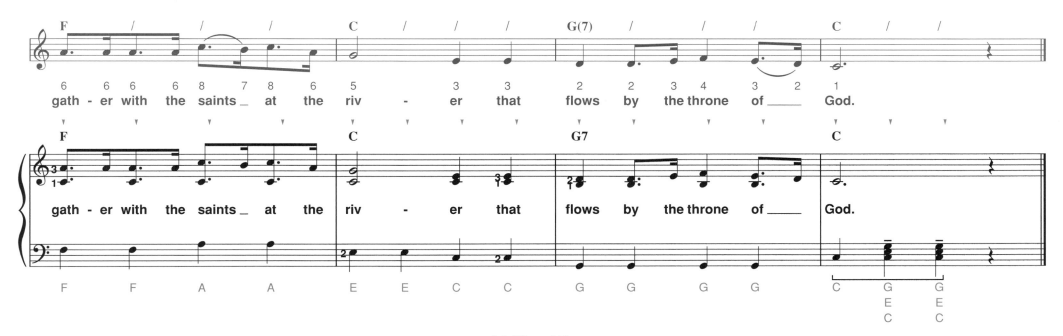

gath - er with the saints _ at the riv - er that flows by the throne of ___ God.

gath - er with the saints _ at the riv - er that flows by the throne of ___ God.

Additional Verses

2. Ere we reach the shining river, lay we ev'ry burden down;
   Grace our spirits will deliver and provide us a robe and a crown.
   (Repeat Chorus)

3. Soon we'll reach the shining river, soon our pilgrimage will cease;
   Soon our happy hearts will quiver with the melody of peace.
   (Repeat Chorus)

What a Difference You've Made in My Life

Words and Music by Archie Jordan

TEMPO: Moderate   RHYTHM: Country or Pops 2   COLOR: Rock or Jazz Organ

One Day at a Time

Words and Music by
Marijohn Wilkins and
Kris Kristofferson

TEMPO: Moderate   RHYTHM: Waltz   COLOR: Rock Organ

SECTION FOUR
Morning Has Broken/Today's Inspirational Favorites

The Greatest Love of All (page 78)
With words by Linda Creed and music by Michael Masser, "The Greatest Love of All" was created for a movie about the life of boxing champion Muhammad Ali (born Cassius Clay) in 1977. The film was called *The Greatest,* after Ali's half-humorous, half-hype description of himself. George Benson, who sang the song on the soundtrack, had a hit with it at the time. Eight years later, Whitney Houston used it as the "B" side of a single and on her debut *Whitney Houston* LP. Enthusiastic radio exposure persuaded her Arista record label to reissue it as an "A" side, and she found herself with a No. 1 hit.

He Touched Me (page 74)
Bill Gaither, born on an Indiana farm, began his career as a high school teacher, but at 25 found a new calling as songwriter and gospel singer. He and his wife, Gloria, have collaborated on a number of gospel favorites, chief among them "He Touched Me," published in 1963, two years after he had established his own music company. It is still among their top successes. More recent hits are "I Am Loved," "A Hill Called Mount Calvary" and "Because He Lives." Bill once wrote, "I have always been very excited by the impact a good song can have on humanity." His enthusiasm bubbles over in this song—a revelation of the feelings he had when Jesus "touched me and made me whole."

Morning Has Broken (page 72)
Eleanor Farjeon (1881–1965), a devout Catholic Englishwoman, was best known for her many children's verses and plays. She began writing at seven and at 16 was co-author of an opera produced at the Royal Academy of Music in London. Even in her lifetime, her work earned the respect of her peers: "a miraculous freshness and originality resembling Mozart's music" was one critic's view. She also was honored by the Queen and won the Hans Christian Andersen and numerous other awards. "Morning Has Broken" is one of several hymn-texts she wrote in 1920, and the words were later coupled with a traditional Gaelic melody. English folksinger Cat Stevens brought the song out of hymnals to a worldwide audience with a major pop hit in 1972.

On Eagle's Wings (page 76)
Michael Joncas, a Roman Catholic priest who has taught theology at the University of St. Thomas in St. Paul, Minnesota, while serving as a parish priest at the same time, adapted the lyrics of "On Eagle's Wings" from Psalm 91, Exodus 19:4 and other Bible verses. He composed the music in 1978, when he was 27 years old, for the funeral service of the father of a friend and fellow seminarian. He later recorded it (accompanying himself on the guitar), as have a number of the song's admirers, among them singer-actor Pat Boone. Besides producing numerous articles and workshops on church music, Father Joncas has published and recorded more than a dozen collections of music for liturgical use and was one of the editors of *Gather,* a hymnal issued by the Gregorian Institute of America.

Reach Out and Touch (Somebody's Hand) (page 83)
Diana Ross, who with the stunningly gifted Supremes accumulated a string of huge hits in the '60s, made her first solo recording with "Reach Out and Touch (Somebody's Hand)," in 1970. The song was written by the husband-and-wife duo of Nikolas Ashford and Valerie Simpson, tunesmiths and producers for Motown Records as well as popular performers in their own right. For her second solo release, Ross chose another Ashford-Simpson song, "Ain't No Mountain High Enough," and shot back into her usual stratospheric orbit with a No. 1 hit.

The Touch of God's Hand (page 91)
The Sons of the Pioneers, one of the best-loved Western singing groups, have enriched the inspirational song repertoire both as a trio and as individuals. For example, one of the founding "Sons," Roy Rogers, went on to become one of America's most popular singing cowboys, starring in more than 90 films. (Roy's wife, Dale Evans, is represented in this songbook by "Happy Trails" and "The Bible Tells Me So.") Another "Son," Tim Spencer, recorded "How Great Thou Art" and started a religious music publishing house, Manna Music, in 1954. The third "Son," Canadian-born Bob Nolan, has composed many cowboy songs that evoke the simplicity and grandeur of the open prairie, among them "Cool Water" and the serene "The Touch of God's Hand."

The Wind Beneath My Wings (page 86)
Although a minor hit for Lou Rawls in early 1983, "The Wind Beneath My Wings," by Larry Henley and Jeff Silbar, first gained a wide audience through Texan singer Gary Morris's country hit later in the year. But the song really became ingrained in the national consciousness via Bette Midler's 1989 chart-topping version, from her hit film *Beaches*—so much so that in a recent poll of America's favorite songs, "The Wind Beneath My Wings" claimed an honored spot among the Top 10.

Morning Has Broken

Words by Eleanor Farjeon; Traditional Gaelic Melody

TEMPO: Moderate   RHYTHM: Waltz   COLOR: (Pan) Flute or Strings

Additional Verses

2. Sweet the rain's new fall, sunlit from Heaven,
   Like the first dew-fall on the first grass.
   Praise for the sweetness of the wet garden,
   Sprung in completeness where His feet pass.

3. Mine is the sunlight, mine is the morning,
   Born of the one light Eden saw play.
   Praise with elation, praise ev'ry morning,
   God's re-creation of the new day.

He Touched Me

Words and Music
by Bill Gaither

TEMPO: Moderately slow   RHYTHM: Waltz or None   COLOR: Organ or Vibraphone

Moderately slow

On Eagle's Wings

Words and Music by Michael Joncas

TEMPO: Moderate   RHYTHM: None*   COLOR: Electric Piano or Flute

*Play each chord where its symbol appears. A "/" means to repeat the preceding chord.

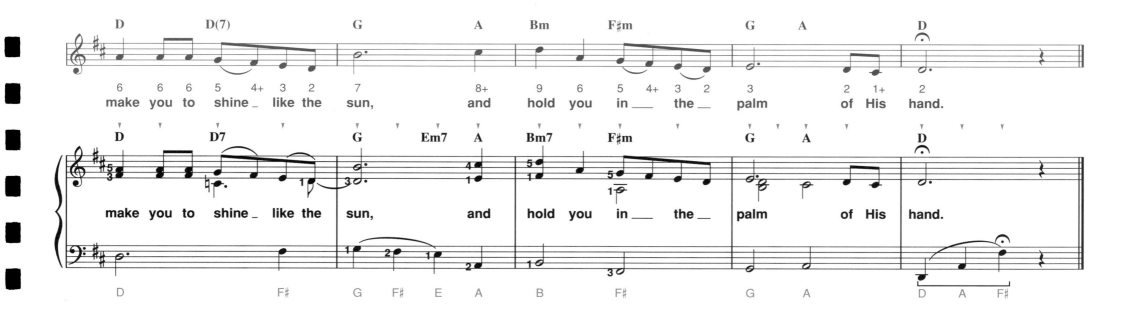

make you to shine _ like the sun, and hold you in ___ the ___ palm of His hand.

make you to shine _ like the sun, and hold you in ___ the ___ palm of His hand.

Additional Verses

2. The snare of the fowler will never capture you,
   And famine will bring you no fear;
   Under His wings your refuge, His faithfulness your shield.
   (Repeat Chorus)

3. You need not fear the terror of the night,
   Nor the arrow that flies by day;
   Though thousands fall about you, near you it shall not come.
   (Repeat Chorus)

4. For to His angels He's given a command
   To guard you in all of your ways;
   Upon their hands they will bear you up, lest you dash your foot against a stone.
   (Repeat Chorus)

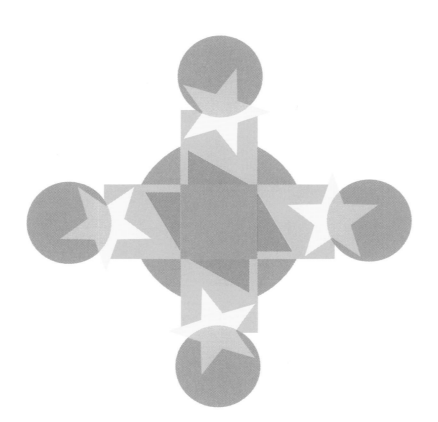

The Greatest Love of All

Words by Linda Creed; Music by Michael Masser

78

Reach Out and Touch
(Somebody's Hand)

Words and Music by Nikolas Ashford and Valerie Simpson

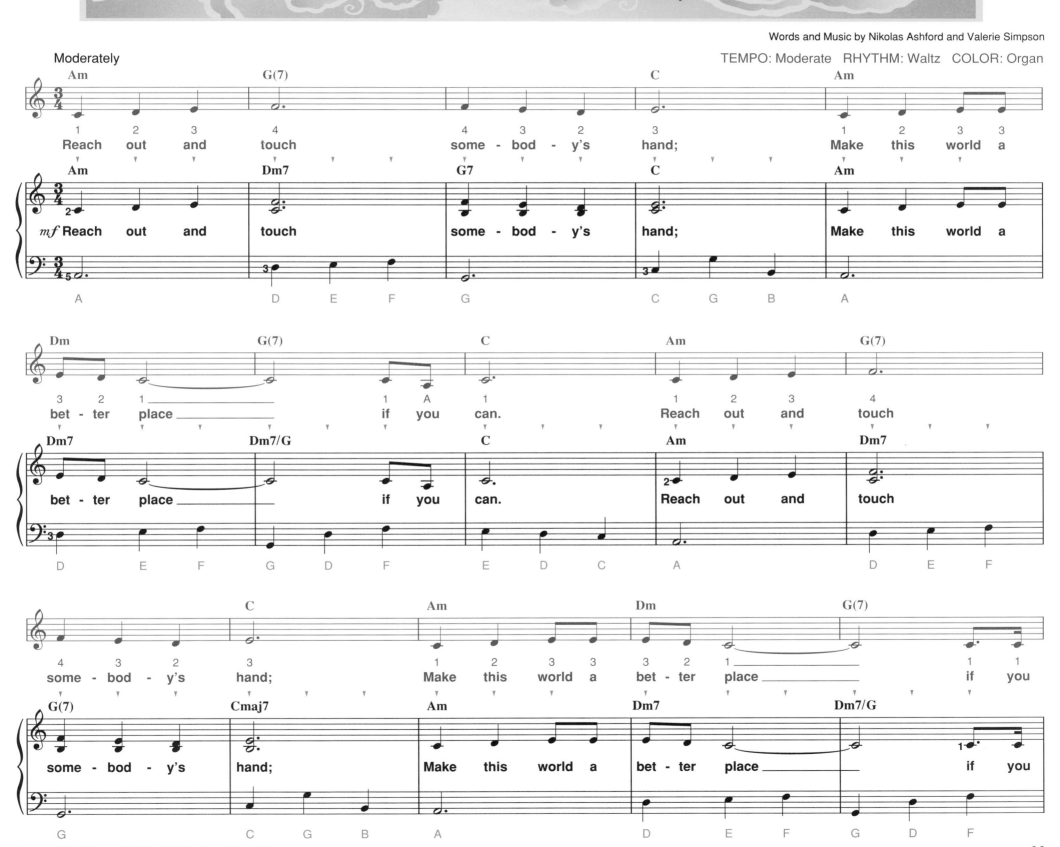

* Play from the beginning
all the way through; use
2nd set of words.

85

The Touch of God's Hand

Words and Music by Bob Nolan

TEMPO: Slow   RHYTHM: Swing   COLOR: Celeste, Vibraphone or Electric Guitar

The prai-rie sun sends down its ray to warm my heart through ev'-ry day; The star-light beam that guides my way is just the touch of God's hand. The scat-tered pearls of morn-ing dew, the rain-bow mists on hills of blue, the sil-ver vale of moon-beams, too, is just the touch of God's hand.

Amazing Grace (page 93)

A one-time vagabond, sailor and slave-trader, John Newton (1725–1807) abandoned his profligate life, after a tumultuous storm at sea nearly sank his vessel, to become an Anglican minister. He kept his congregation in awe with his stentorian voice, his hellfire-and-brimstone beliefs, his habit of preaching in his sea captain's uniform and his dramatic poetry and hymn-texts. "Amazing Grace" is one of these. It was first published, with the anonymous tune sung today, in the American "shape-note" hymnal *The Virginia Harmony* in 1831. ("Shape notes" refer to notes in different shapes—diamonds, flags, squares, triangles, circles—for those who couldn't read music.) Long a favorite in churches throughout the land, the hymn found a new audience in 1971, when Judy Collins' recording, backed by a cathedral choir, became a Top 15 pop hit. A year later, an "amazing" version by The Royal Scots Dragoon Guards—with a full complement of bagpipes, of course—further cemented its popularity.

Can the Circle Be Unbroken (page 102)

Ada Habershon, an Englishwoman, became known in the United States through her dedicated participation in revival meetings led by such distinguished evangelists as Ira Sankey (himself a noted gospel songwriter) and Dwight Moody. There she encountered a kindred soul, the musician Charles Gabriel, among whose religious ditties was "Brighten the Corner Where You Are" (see page 152). Eager to try her hand, Habershon wrote the words and Gabriel the music for "Will the Circle Be Unbroken," published in 1907 and soon a gospel staple. Probably based on his recollections of the hymn as a child, A.P. Carter in 1935 altered the tune, words and title (changing it to "*Can* the Circle Be Unbroken") to create a more folklike piece for The Carter Family, the famous country group of which he was the founding patriarch. His version, recorded in May that year, was widely imitated thereafter and is the one included in this songbook.

He's Got the Whole World in His Hands (page 101)

Though probably a century and a half old (nobody knows its age exactly), this African-American spiritual was not actually written down and published until sometime between 1927 and 1935 (even that date is uncertain), when it was "collected" by a folk-song enthusiast named Frank Warner. The late contralto Marian Anderson shares honors with gospel artist Mahalia Jackson for promoting the song to world fame. Beginning in the '30s, Anderson sang it so often on her concert tours all over the globe that it became a kind of theme song for her. In the '50s, Jackson imbued it with her particular gospel style and earned millions of new admirers. A 1958 British recording of "He's Got the Whole World" by 13-year-old Laurie London soared to No. 1 on the pop lists and stayed at the top of the charts for four weeks.

If I Had a Hammer (page 94)

Pete Seeger's career in folk music has been long and distinguished, dating from his solo concerts in the '30s and '40s, and encompassing his years with The Weavers, a singing group he organized with Lee Hays, Ronnie Gilbert and Fred Hellerman. The Weavers, whose biggest hit was "Good Night, Irene" in 1950, recorded "If I Had a Hammer," written by Seeger and Hays, in 1958. Peter, Paul and Mary's 1962 hit version and Trini Lopez's gently Latin-styled 1963 recording kept "The Hammer Song," as it is also called, at the forefront of the folk movement.

Michael, Row the Boat Ashore (page 105)

Folk enthusiasts discovered this tune in the Sea Islands off the Georgia coast and surmised that it originated as a work song sung by the crews on plantation riverboats—and thus is a kind of sea chantey. The music was printed by Charles Ware as early as 1867 in his *Slave Songs of the United States*, though it had been in common use long before that. "Michael" is the Archangel Michael, whose grace was implored when the load was particularly heavy or the tide especially strong. Harry Belafonte had a notable recording of the song in the '50s, and the folk quintet The Highwaymen revived it as a No. 1 hit in 1961.

Put Your Hand in the Hand (page 96)

Gene MacLellan's résumé includes stints as a busboy, farmer and hospital worker, but probably the experience that most buoyed up this Canadian-born songwriter was his time spent as musical accompanist to a traveling evangelist. Now one of Prince Edward Island's best-known citizens (he prefers the rustic solitude there to the faster pace of Toronto), he admits to a certain fundamentalism in his own beliefs. They are echoed in this gospel song, which was picked up by fellow Canadian superstar Anne Murray and recorded in 1970. Her sizable success was eclipsed by that of the vocal group Ocean, who took the song to the No. 2 spot in 1971.

Turn! Turn! Turn! (To Everything There Is a Season) (page 98)

Pete Seeger, along with the folk missionaries Leadbelly, Woody Guthrie, Lee Hays and Odetta, has sung authentic American folk songs for so many years that his own compositions resemble them. He wrote "Turn! Turn! Turn!" in 1962, basing the text on verses of the third chapter of the Bible's Book of Ecclesiastes; the three "turn's" of the title are in fact the only nonbiblical words. Though the song was recorded by The Weavers (Seeger, Hays, Fred Hillerman and Ronnie Gilbert), the most successful disk was that of The Byrds in 1965—their second No. 1 hit after "Mr. Tambourine Man."

Wondrous Love (page 104)

The words and music of this beautiful hymn, whose original sources are unknown, are found in several 19th-century shape-note hymnals. One such songbook was Baptist layman William Walker's *The Southern Harmony and Musical Companion* (1835), the most prevalent shape-note collection in the Deep South. According to Walker, "Wondrous Love" was one of the most popular folk hymns of the day, sung throughout the South and Midwest as far north as the Dakota Territory. The hymn also appeared in *The Harp of Columbia* (1848).

AMAZING GRACE

Words by John Newton; Music Traditional

TEMPO: Slow   RHYTHM: Waltz   COLOR: Bagpipe*, Strings or Pipe Organ

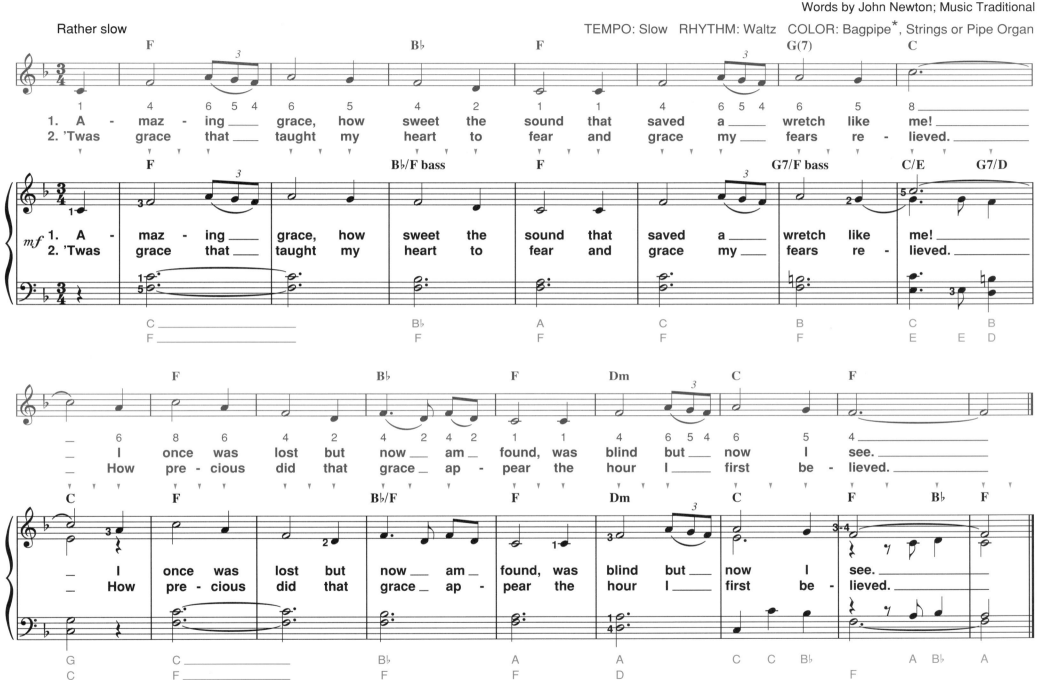

*Note: To simulate a true bagpipe effect, hold the F and C down with the left hand and play the melody in single notes with the right hand.

Additional Verses

3. Through many dangers, toils and snares
I have already come;
'Tis grace hath brought me safe thus far,
And grace will lead me home.

4. The Lord has promised good to me,
His word my hope secures;
He will my shield and portion be
As long as life endures.

If I Had a Hammer

Words and Music by Lee Hays and Pete Seeger

Moderate rock beat

TEMPO: Moderate   RHYTHM: Rock 'n' Roll   COLOR: Rock Organ, Accordion

1. If I had a ham - mer, I'd ham - mer in the morn - ing,
2. If I had a bell, I'd ring it in the morn - ing,

I'd ham - mer in the eve - ning all o - ver this land.
I'd ring it in the eve - ning all o - ver this land.

I'd ham - mer out dan - ger, I'd ham - mer out a warn - ing,
I'd ring out dan - ger, I'd ring out a warn - ing,

Additional Verses

3. If I had a song, I'd sing it in the morning,
   I'd sing it in the evening all over this land.
   I'd sing out danger, I'd sing out a warning,
   I'd sing out love between my brothers and my sisters
   All over this land.

4. Well, I got a hammer, and I've got a bell,
   And I've got a song all over this land.
   It's the hammer of justice, it's the bell of freedom,
   It's the song about love between my brothers and my sisters,
   All over this land.

Put Your Hand in the Hand

Words and Music by Gene MacLellan

TEMPO: Moderate   RHYTHM: Swing   COLOR: Jazz Organ

Moderately, with a swing

Put your hand in the hand of the man who stilled the wa-ter. Put your hand in the hand of the man who calmed the sea. Take a look at your-self and-a you can look at oth-ers dif-f'rent-ly by put-tin' your hand in the hand of the man from-a Gal-i-lee. Ev-'ry time I look in-to the Ma-ma taught me how to pray be-fore I

Turn! Turn! Turn!
(To Everything There Is a Season)

Words from the Book of Ecclesiastes;
Music by Pete Seeger

TEMPO: Moderate   RHYTHM: Pops   COLOR: Harpsichord, Guitar

99

He's Got the Whole World in His Hands

Traditional

TEMPO: Moderate   RHYTHM: Big Band/Swing   COLOR: Rock organ, Synth–reed

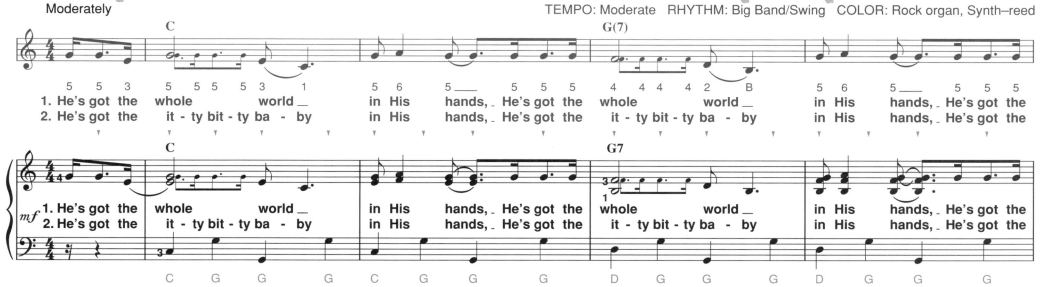

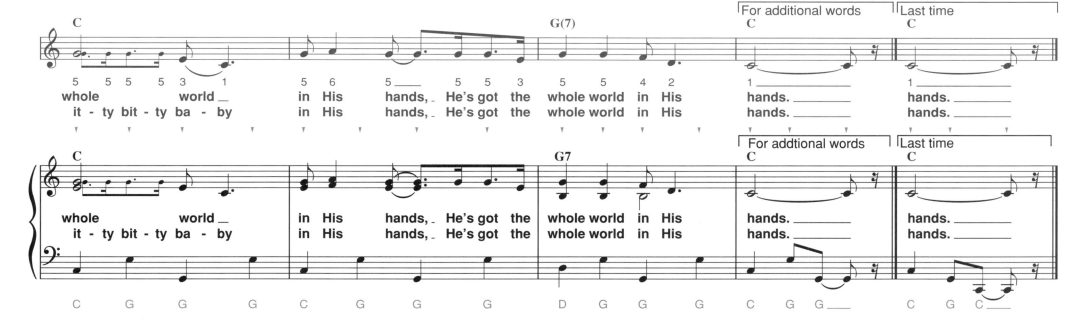

Additional Verses

3. He's got-a you and me, brother, in His hands,
   He's got-a you and me, brother, in His hands,
   He's got-a you and me, brother, in His hands,
   He's got the whole world in His hands.

(Continue similarly)

4. He's got-a you and me, sister . . .

5. He's got the rambler and the gambler . . .

6. He's got the grifter and the grafter . . .

7. He's got the rounder and the bounder . . .

8. He's got the whole world . . .

Can the Circle Be Unbroken

Words and Music by A.P. Carter

TEMPO: Moderate   RHYTHM: Country or Slow Rock   COLOR: Harmonica or (Reed) Organ

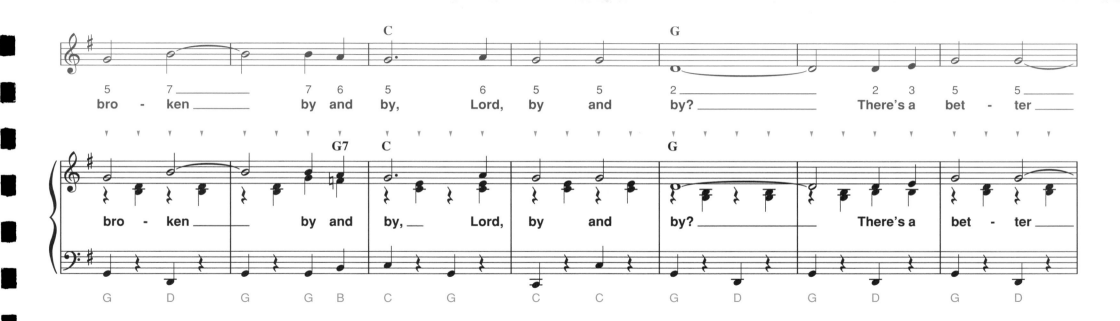

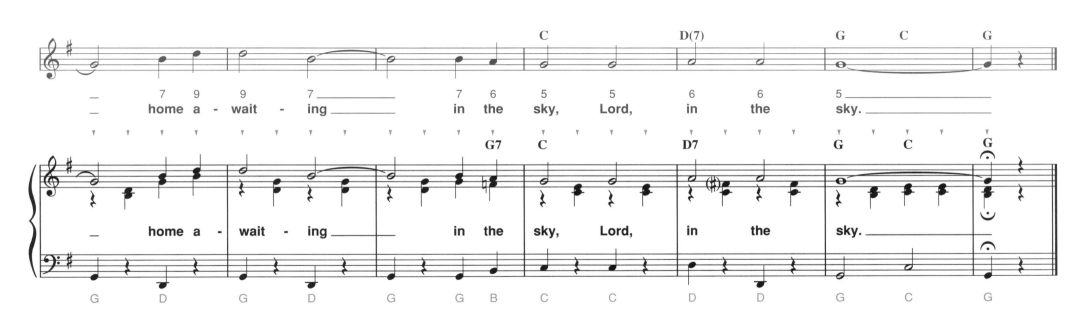

Additional Verses

2. Yes, I followed close behind her,
   Tried to cheer up and be brave,
   But my sorrows, I could not hide them
   When they laid her in the grave.
   (Repeat Chorus)

3. Went back home, Lord, cold and lonesome,
   Since my mother, she was gone.
   All my brothers and sisters crying,
   What a home, so sad and lone.
   (Repeat Chorus)

WONDROUS LOVE

Traditional

*Play each chord where its symbol appears. A "/" means to repeat the previous chord.

Michael, Row the Boat Ashore

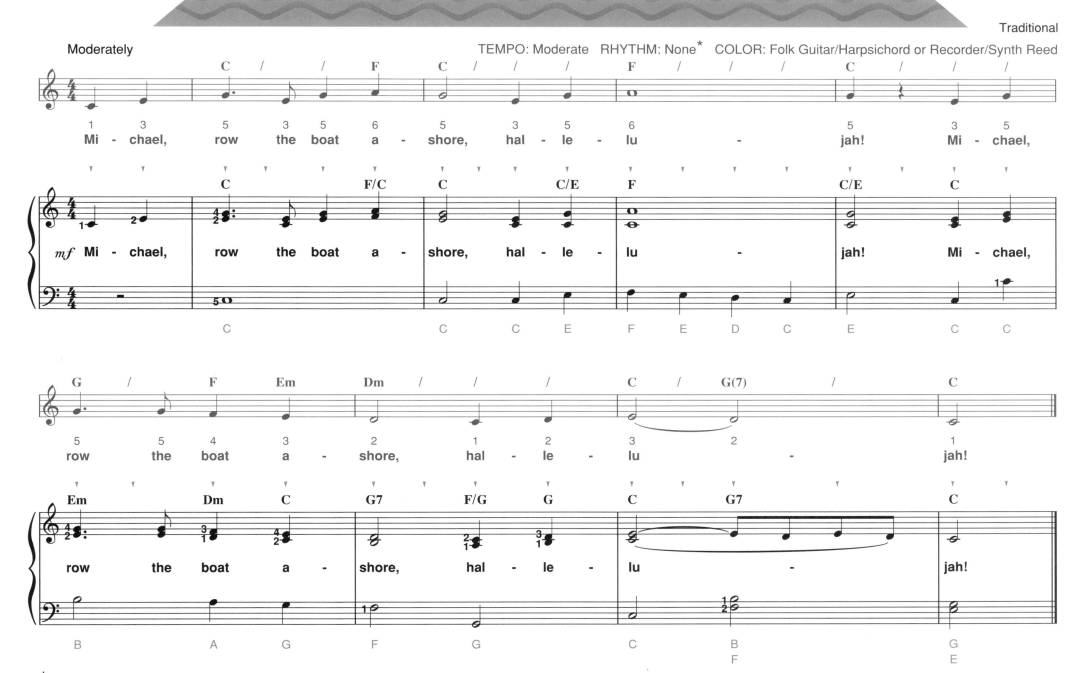

Traditional

Moderately

TEMPO: Moderate   RHYTHM: None*   COLOR: Folk Guitar/Harpsichord or Recorder/Synth Reed

* Play each chord where its symbol appears. A "/" means to repeat the previous chord.

Additional Verses

2. Sister, help to trim the sails, hallelujah!
   Sister, help to trim the sails, hallelujah!

3. Brother, help to stroke the oars, hallelujah!
   Brother, help to stroke the oars, hallelujah!

4. Jordan River is deep and wide, hallelujah!
   Meet my Savior on the other side, hallelujah!

SECTION SIX
We Sing His Praises/Songs of Adoration Addressed to the Lord

His Name Is Wonderful (page 112)
On Christmas Day, 1956, Audrey Mieir was sitting in the choir loft of a church whose pastorate she and her husband, both ordained ministers, were then sharing with her husband's brother and his wife. She was so moved at the sermon being preached by her brother-in-law, the beauty of the children's faces and the obvious presence of the Christmas spirit that, when the famous lines from Isaiah 9:6, "His name shall be called Wonderful," were quoted, she was inspired to jot down in the flyleaf of a Bible her own poem of adoration and a melody to accompany it—all in a matter of minutes. "Purely praise from my heart" is how she describes it.

Holy God, We Praise Thy Name (page 114)
The tune is believed to have come from an ancient setting of the *Te Deum* ("We Praise Thee"), a canticle or song chanted in the early days of the Christian church, perhaps as early as the third century. Clarence Augustus Walworth (1820–1900), a Catholic rector in Albany, New York, translated the words from a German hymnal belonging to Maria Theresa, empress of Austria in the 18th century, though the lyrics undoubtedly date from much earlier. Walworth was trained as a lawyer, but decided to devote himself to religion instead and became a mission preacher of remarkable eloquence. He later went blind, yet in his last decade continued to praise God's name in gratitude for the faith that had afforded him such joy for so long.

How Great Thou Art (page 108)
George Beverly Shea, a featured singer with the Billy Graham Crusades for many years, heard what would soon become his most frequently requested religious solo in London in the 1950s. An English publisher introduced it to him, noting that the text and music had originated with a 25-year-old Swedish minister, Carl Boberg, in 1886. A Russian translation of the words were discovered in the Ukraine by an English clergyman, Stuart Hine, who used to sing "How Great Thou Art" with his wife at worship services and other gatherings. Hine translated the text into English, adding a fourth stanza. Over the years, hundreds of recordings of the song have been made, but "Bev" Shea's first, made in 1954, is still among the most popular.

I Need Thee Ev'ry Hour (page 111)
Annie Sherwood began writing religious poems when she was only a girl in upstate New York. Later, she married a young man named Hawks and moved to Brooklyn, where she became a member of a Baptist church whose pastor was Robert Lowry, the renowned preacher, publisher and composer of gospel songs, including "Shall We Gather at the River?" (see page 62). Lowry, delighted by Annie Sherwood Hawks's poetic talent, encouraged her to concentrate on hymns, for which he often supplied the music. Their best-known collaboration is "I Need Thee Ev'ry Hour," written in 1872. Hawks once confessed that she had never understood the widespread appeal of her hymn until she herself experienced a severe loss and discovered the spiritual comfort inherent in the words that she "had been allowed to write."

Jesu, Joy of Man's Desiring (page 118)
Johann Sebastian Bach's lovely chorus comes from his Cantata No. 147, *Herz und Mund und Tat und Leben* (Heart and Mouth and Deed and Life), composed in 1716 for the Duke of Weimar, in whose chapel Bach worked between 1704 and 1717. The Duke was very demanding, with a sour disposition and drab personality to boot. So severe a disciplinarian was he that when Bach received the offer of a far better job a few villages away, the Duke was so offended that he had the Court Marshall put Bach in detention for three weeks. "Jesu, Joy of Man's Desiring" has as its text a biblical paraphrase translated by Catherine Drinker Bowen, while the melody is based on a 1642 Lutheran chorale. We use only the melody here.

Joyful, Joyful, We Adore Thee (page 120)
The tune for this hymn comes from the last movement of the magnificent Ninth, or "Choral," Symphony of Ludwig van Beethoven. The melody is one of the most perfect he ever composed, although he had been totally deaf for almost two decades when he wrote it in 1824 (three years before his death). The words we sing to the tune have nothing to do with the original German text, a nonsacred "Ode to Joy" by Friedrich von Schiller. The English text is the work of Philadelphia-born Henry Van Dyke, successively a beloved and influential preacher at the historic Brick Presbyterian Church in New York City, an ambassador to the Netherlands and a professor of English at Princeton University.

A Mighty Fortress Is Our God (page 116)
One of the most stalwart religious tunes in Christianity, probably the work of the founder of the Reformation, Martin Luther, is combined with an equally strong text, also Luther's, written sometime between 1521 and 1534, when he was laboring to translate the Bible into German. It is based on a verse of Psalm 46 and is believed to have been first published in 1529, though no copy of the original publication or the manuscript exists. Many English translations have appeared over the years, but the one most commonly used is by Frederic Henry Hedge, first printed in 1842 in the English collection *Hymns for the Church of Christ*.

My Faith Looks Up to Thee (page 107)
In 1830, when Yale graduate and budding poet Ray Palmer sat down to write his first hymn, he was nearly overcome. As he put it, "Christ, in the riches of His grace and love, was so vividly apprehended as to fill [me] with deep emotion." He also noted that, as he penned the final line about "a ransomed soul," he was moved "to abundant tears." Not long afterwards, leading hymnist Lowell Mason asked Palmer if he had anything that could be set to music, and Palmer produced these verses. Mason read them and said to him, "You may live many years, but I think you will be best known for these lines." Mason had been educated as a banker, but his religious convictions persuaded him to take up the cause of church music, which he pursued with vigor and scrupulous musical taste. Organists and choir directors are still in his debt.

My Faith Looks Up to Thee

Music by Ray Palmer ; Words by Lowell Mason

TEMPO: Moderate   RHYTHM: None   COLOR: Organ

Additional Verses

3. While life's dark maze I tread
And griefs around me spread,
Be Thou my guide.
Bid darkness turn to day,
Wipe sorrow's tears away,
Nor let me ever stray
From Thee aside.

4. When ends life's transient dream
When death's cold sullen stream
Shall o'er me roll,
Blest Savior then in love,
Fear and distrust remove,
O bear me safe above
A ransomed soul.

How Great Thou Art

Music by Carl Boberg; English Words by Stuart K. Hine

TEMPO: Slow   RHYTHM: None   COLOR: Organ

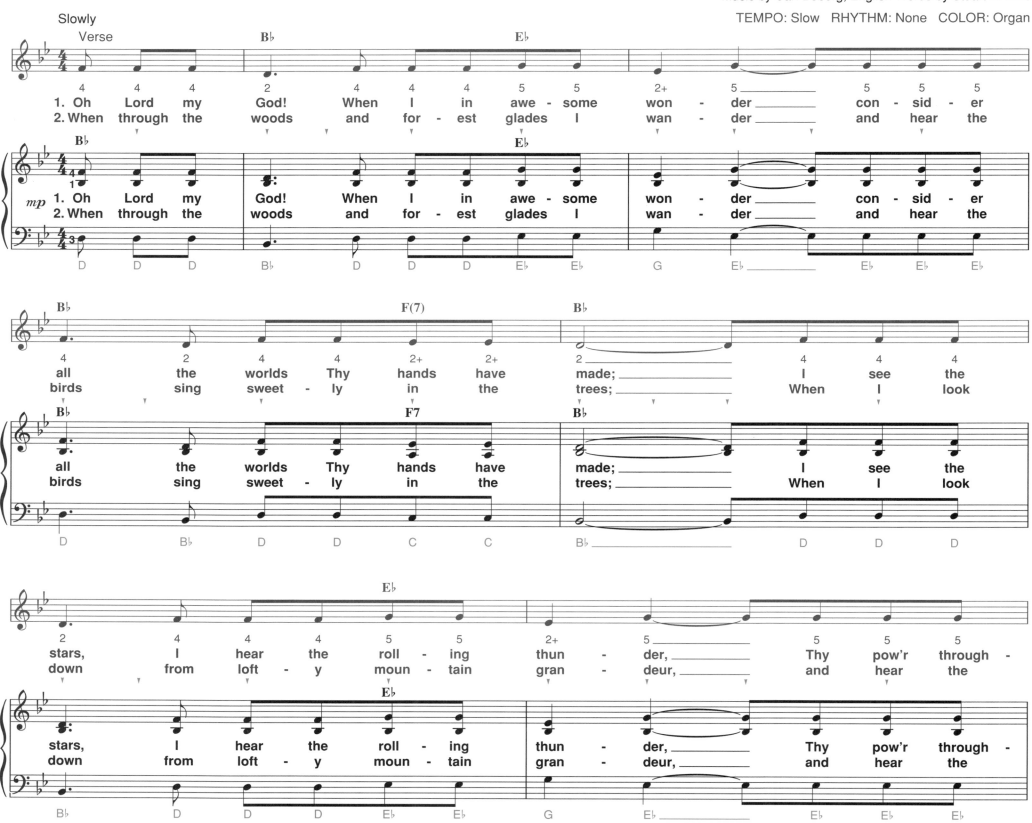

Additional Verses

3. And when I think that God, His Son not sparing,
   Sent Him to die, I scarce can take it in;
   That on the cross my burden gladly bearing,
   He bled and died to take away my sin.
   (Repeat Chorus)

4. When Christ shall come with shout of acclamation
   And take me home, what joy shall fill my heart!
   Then I shall bow in humble adoration
   And there proclaim: My God, how great Thou art!
   (Repeat Chorus)

I Need Thee Ev'ry Hour

Words by Annie Sherwood Hawks; Music by the Rev. Robert Lowry

TEMPO: Moderate   RHYTHM: None   COLOR: Organ

Additional Verses

3. I need Thee ev'ry hour,
   In joy or pain;
   Come quickly and abide,
   Or life is vain.
   (Repeat Chorus)

4. I need Thee ev'ry hour,
   Teach me Thy will;
   And Thy rich promises
   In me fulfill.
   (Repeat Chorus)

His Name Is Wonderful

Words and Music by
Audrey Mieir

TEMPO: Moderately slow   RHYTHM: Waltz   COLOR: Celeste/Vibraphone

Holy God, We Praise Thy Name

English Words by Clarence Walworth; Music Traditional

TEMPO: Moderate   RHYTHM: Waltz or None   COLOR: Organ

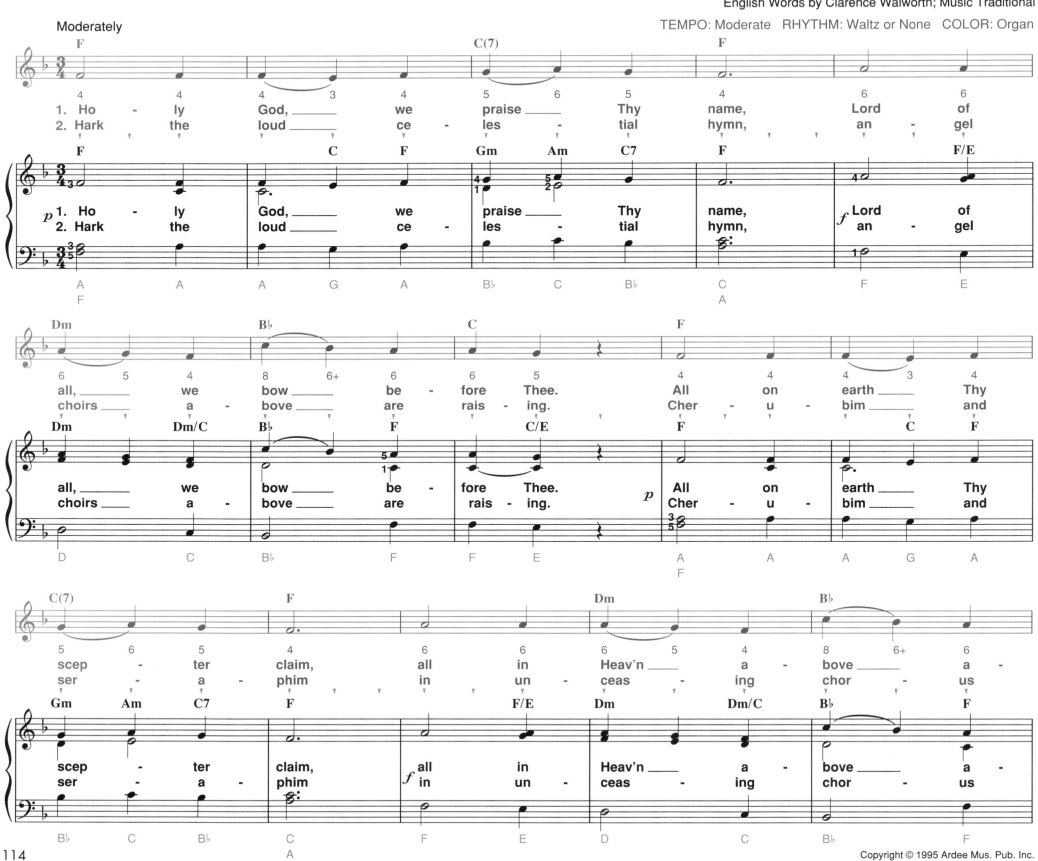

114

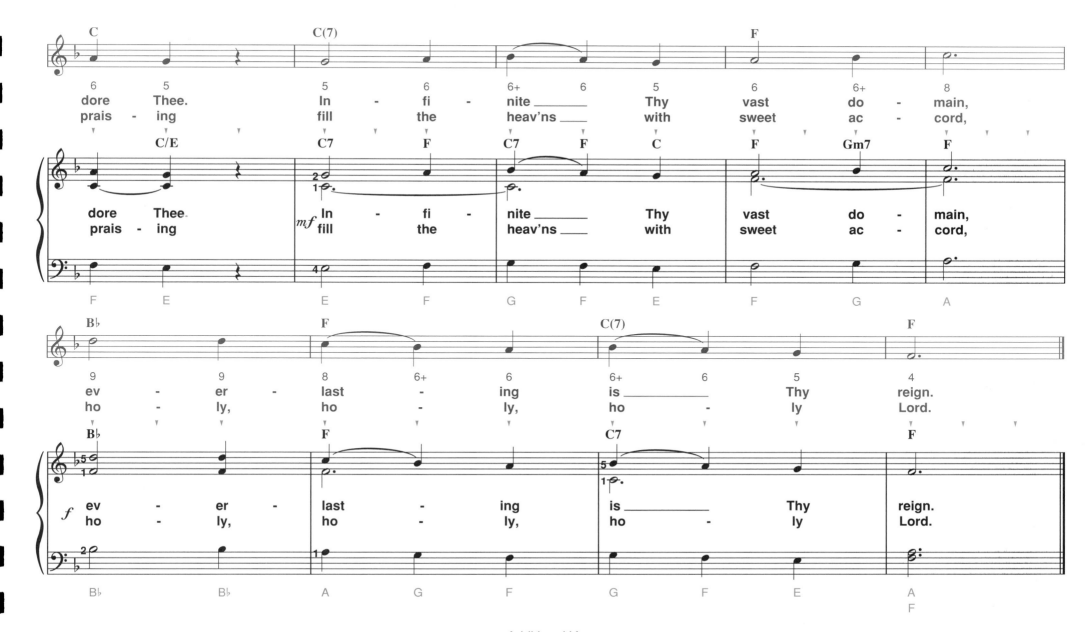

Additional Verses

3. Lo, the apostolic train
   Joins Thy sacred name to hallow.
   Prophets swell the glad refrain,
   And the white-robed martyrs follow.
   And from morn to set of sun
   Through the church the song goes on.

4. Holy Father, Holy Son,
   Holy Spirit, Three we name Thee.
   While in essence only one,
   Undivided God we claim Thee.
   And adoring bend the knee,
   While we sing our praise to Thee.

A Mighty Fortress Is Our God

German Words and Music
by Martin Luther;
English Translation
by Frederick H. Hedge

Maestoso (majestically, without dragging)

TEMPO: Moderate   RHYTHM: None*   COLOR: (Pipe) Organ

* Play each chord where its symbol appears. A "/" means to repeat the preceding chord.

Jesu, Joy of Man's Desiring

Music by
Johann Sebastian Bach

In a slow 3 (each ♩ = one beat)　　　　　TEMPO: Very slow　　RHYTHM: None　　COLOR: Street Organ, Flute or Strings

118

Joyful, Joyful, We Adore Thee

English Words by Henry van Dyke; Music by Ludwig van Beethoven

TEMPO: Moderately fast   RHYTHM: None*   COLOR: Organ

* Play each chord where its symbol appears. A "/" means to repeat the preceding chord.

Additional Verses

2. All Thy works with joy surround Thee,
   Earth and Heaven reflect Thy rays,
   Stars and angels sing around Thee,
   Center of unbroken praise:
   Field and forest, vale and mountain,
   Blooming meadow, flashing sea,
   Chanting bird and flowing fountain,
   Call us to rejoice in Thee.

3. Thou art giving and forgiving,
   Ever blessing, ever blest,
   Wellspring of the joy of living,
   Ocean depth of happy rest!
   Thou our Father, Christ our brother,
   All who live in love are Thine:
   Teach us how to love each other,
   Lift us to the joy divine.

4. Mortals join the mighty chorus,
   Which the morning stars began;
   Father love is reigning o'er us,
   Brother love binds man to man.
   Ever singing march we onward,
   Victors in the midst of strife;
   Joyful music lifts us sunward
   In the triumph song of life.

Bringing In the Sheaves (page 134)

A young man who had entered the ministry at age 19 wrote the words for this all-time favorite revival hymn. Knowles Shaw based his text on some verses from Psalm 126: "They that sow in tears shall reap in joy. He that goeth forth and weepeth, bearing precious seed, shall doubtless come again with rejoicing, bringing his sheaves with him." How his poem came to be teamed with George A. Minor's hearty four-square tune is now lost in the dusty lore of the evangelical gospel meetings that formed such an important part of religious life in rural America in the late 19th century.

His Eye Is on the Sparrow (page 132)

Stillman and Celia Martin were a team of evangelists who preached, prayed and waxed poetic in the early years of the 20th century. One of Mrs. Martin's poems impressed her husband so much that, rather than bury its beauty under mundane music of his own, he sought a musical setting from the premier gospel-hymn composer of the time, Charles H. Gabriel. Thus came about the imperishable melody for "His Eye Is on the Sparrow," made famous not only by revival-meeting preachers but by Ethel Waters singing it each night in Carson McCullers' 1950 drama *The Member of the Wedding*. Miss Waters later used the song's title for her autobiography.

Holy, Holy, Holy (page 129)

Reginald Heber, an English bishop who served his church in Calcutta, India, died of apoplexy there at age 43 in 1826, the same year he wrote one of Christianity's finest hymns, "Holy, Holy, Holy." These verses, occasioned by his fellow-cleric father-in-law's request, honored the Holy Trinity—Father, Son and Holy Ghost. His words found an eloquent and appropriate setting in the John B. Dykes tune "Nicaea," written especially for them in 1861 and named for the church council of Nicaea at which the doctrine of the Trinity was clearly defined in A.D. 325.

Lead, Kindly Light (page 126)

John Henry Newman, the Anglican theologian and later Roman Catholic cardinal, found himself on a becalmed boat between Corsica and Sardinia one hot June day in 1833. As the crew waited for a saving breeze, he wrote the verses of "Lead, Kindly Light" that likened their plight to that of the soul waiting for the reviving breath of God. He later described his poem as "humble" and modestly attributed its subsequent popularity to the tune composed for it by John Bacchus Dykes. Music and verse were first published in the 1861 edition of *Hymns Ancient and Modern*.

The Little Brown Church in the Vale (page 122)

The church immortalized in this song still stands near Nashua, Iowa, in a vale of trees now grown taller than its bell tower. Pioneers built it in 1864, contributing all the timber, stone and labor themselves. William S. Pitts, a country doctor and music teacher, saw in the serenity of the site such a striking testament to faith that he penned this tribute. The song, also called "The Church in the Wildwood," has made the little church so widely known that, when it was to be torn down in 1888, admirers who knew it because of Pitts's tune banded together to preserve it.

Love Divine, All Loves Excelling (page 128)

The brothers Charles and John Wesley not only founded Methodism (by their investigation of the "methods" of the Anglican Church) but between them wrote more than 6,500 hymns, at least 500 of which, including "Love Divine, All Loves Excelling," are in frequent use today. The words of this hymn are by Charles and were first published in *Hymns for Those Who Seek* in 1756. But it was not until 1849 that organist John Zundel composed this masterly setting and named the melody after the Rev. Henry Ward Beecher, brother of author Harriet Beecher Stowe.

Nearer, My God, to Thee (page 137)

Sarah Fuller Adams, a prominent English religious poet and Unitarian, wrote the text of "Nearer, My God, to Thee" in 1840. She based it on Jacob's dream at Bethel described in Genesis 28:12–15, wherein he sees "a ladder set up on the earth, and the top of it reached to heaven." (See also "Jacob's Ladder," described on page 147.) Lowell Mason's music for the hymn concerned no dream. On the contrary, as he himself wrote, "One night after lying awake in the dark, eyes wide open, through the stillness in the house the melody came to me, and the next morning I wrote it down." The words and music were first published together in 1859.

The Old Rugged Cross (page 124)

Often known as the world's favorite gospel hymn, "The Old Rugged Cross" was written by the Rev. George Bennard while he was "praying for a full understanding of the cross and its plan in Christianity." The melody came to him easily, he said, but when he found his mind stubbornly stuck on the phrase "old rugged cross," a voice within bade him wait to finish the poem. Months passed until finally, in 1913, a series of triumphant revival meetings gave him the inspiration he needed. The hymn was made famous by Homer Rodeheaver, the evangelist, singer, trombonist and music publisher.

Rock of Ages (page 136)

The power of its poetic image has made this hymn by Augustus Montague Toplady a source of personal strength and faith for millions. Toplady, an English-born Calvinist minister, published a shorter version of his stanzas in *Gospel* magazine in 1776, using as a comparison, surprisingly, the British national debt: like fiscal obligations, our sins, unchecked, can multiply fatally. The American hymnist Thomas Hastings composed the musical setting, as widely admired as the words, and published it in *Spiritual Songs for Social Worship* in 1833.

What a Friend We Have in Jesus (page 130)

The day before their wedding, Joseph Scriven's fiancée accidentally drowned. Grief-stricken, he emigrated from Ireland to Canada and spent his life among the Plymouth Brethren, ministering to the aged. In 1855, trying to comfort his mother back in Ireland, he wrote the verses of "What a Friend We Have in Jesus" and let them be published anonymously. Even when his authorship was discovered, he modestly tried to share it: "The Lord and I did it between us," he said. Charles Converse, a Pennsylvania attorney and pipe-organ enthusiast, contributed the tune in 1870.

The Little Brown Church in the Vale

Words and Music by William S. Pitts

Moderately and very steady (Play chords once for each beat)

TEMPO: Moderate   RHYTHM: March or None   COLOR: Organ or Brass Synth

Additional Verses

2. How sweet on a clear Sabbath morning,
   To list to the clear ringing bell;
   Its tones so sweetly are calling,
   O come to the church in the vale.
   (Repeat Chorus)

3. From the church in the valley by the wildwood
   When day fades away into night,
   I would fain from this spot of my childhood
   Wing my way to the mansions of light.
   (Repeat Chorus)

The Old Rugged Cross

Words and Music by the Rev. George Bennard

TEMPO: Moderate   RHYTHM: Waltz or None   COLOR: Organ or Strings

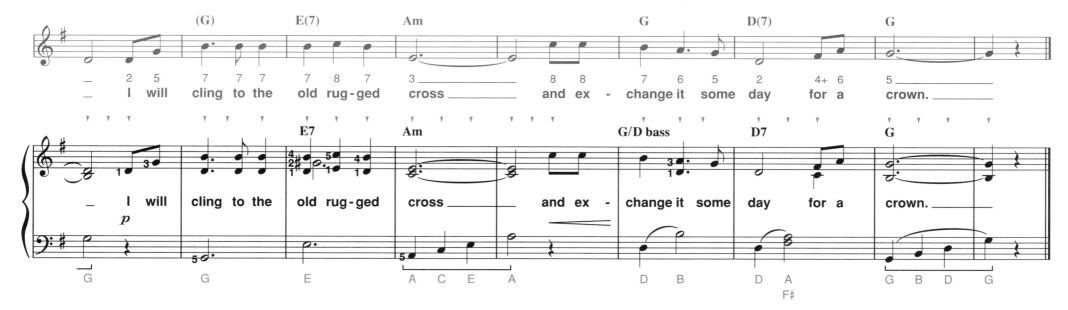

Additional Verses

2. Oh, that old rugged cross so despised by the world
   Has a wondrous attraction for me,
   For the dear Lamb of God left His glory above
   To bear it to dark Calvary.
   (Repeat Chorus)

3. In the old rugged cross, stained with blood so divine,
   A wondrous beauty I see.
   For 'twas on that old cross Jesus suffered and died
   To pardon and sanctify me.
   (Repeat Chorus)

4. To the old rugged cross I will ever be true,
   Its shame and reproach gladly bear,
   Then He'll call me some day to my home far away,
   Where His glory forever I'll share.
   (Repeat Chorus)

Lead, Kindly Light

Words by John Henry Newman; Music by John B. Dykes

TEMPO: Rather slow   RHYTHM: None   COLOR: Organ

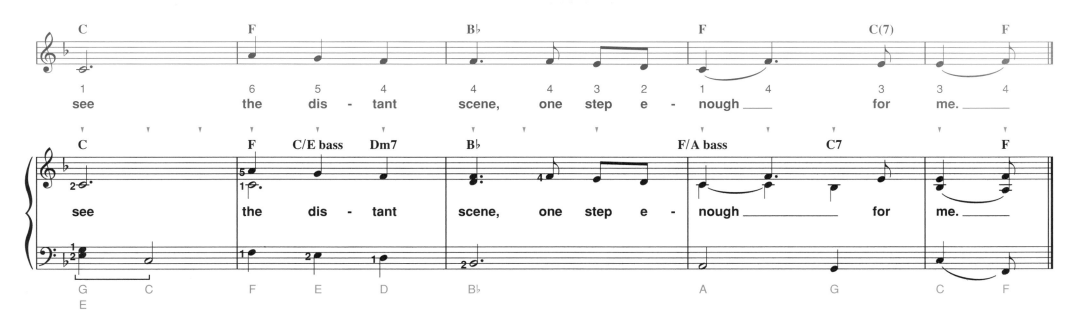

Additional Verses

2. I was not ever thus nor prayed that Thou
   Shouldst lead me on.
   I loved to choose and see my path, but now
   Lead Thou me on.
   I loved the garish day and spite of fears,
   Pride ruled my will; Remember not past years.

3. So long Thy pow'r hath blest me, sure it still
   Will lead me on.
   O'er moor and fen, o'er crag and torrent till
   The night is gone.
   And with the morn those angel faces smile,
   Which I have loved long since and lost a while.

Love Divine, All Loves Excelling

Words by Charles Wesley; Music by John Zundel

TEMPO: Moderate   RHYTHM: None   COLOR: Organ

Additional Verses

2. Breathe, O breathe Thy loving spirit
Into ev'ry troubled breast!
Let us all in Thee inherit,
Let us find that promised rest.
Take away the love of sinning,
Alpha and Omega be;
End of faith, as its beginning,
Set our hearts at liberty!

3. Come, Almighty, to deliver,
Let us all Thy life receive;
Suddenly return and never,
Nevermore Thy temples leave;
Thee we would be always blessing,
Serve Thee as Thy hosts above,
Pray and praise Thee without ceasing,
Glory inThy perfect love!

4. Finish then Thy new creation,
Pure and spotless may we be;
Let us see our whole salvation,
Perfectly secured in Thee.
Changed from glory into glory,
Till in Heav'n we take our place,
Till we cast our crowns before Thee,
Lost in wonder, love and praise!

Holy, Holy, Holy

Words by Reginald Heber;
Music by John B. Dykes

TEMPO: Moderate   RHYTHM: None   COLOR: Organ

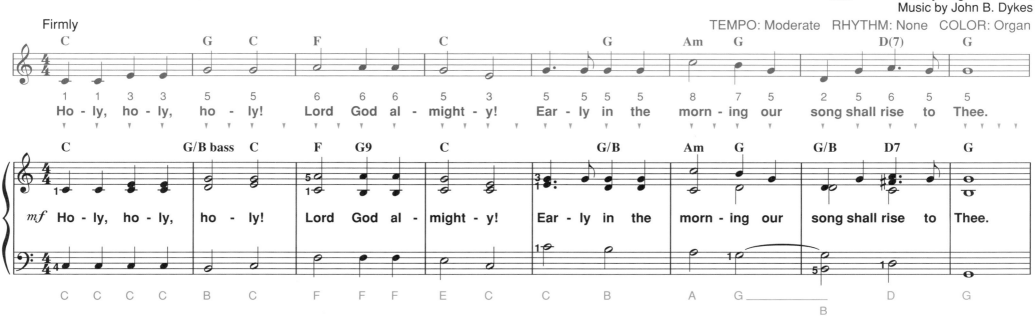

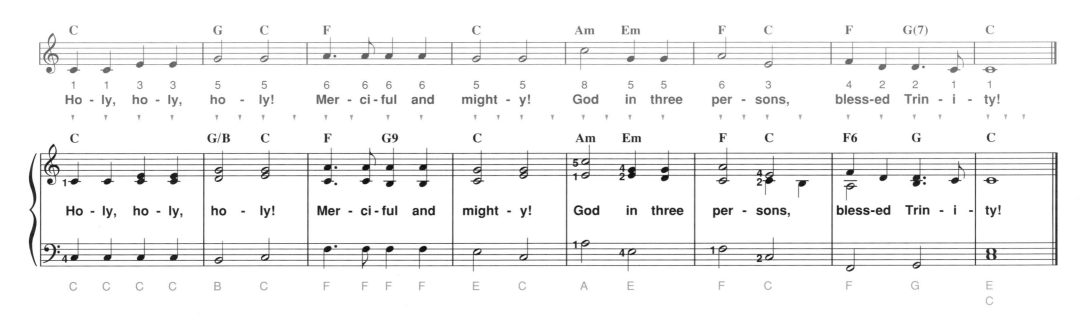

Additional Verses

2. Holy, holy, holy! All the saints adore Thee,
   Casting down their golden crowns around the glassy sea.
   Cherubim and seraphim, falling down before Thee,
   Which wert and art and evermore shall be.

3. Holy, holy, holy! Lord God Almighty!
   All Thy works shall praise Thy name in earth and sky and sea.
   Holy, holy, holy! Merciful and mighty!
   God in three persons, blessed Trinity!

What a Friend We Have in Jesus

Words by Joseph Scriven;
Music by Charles C. Converse

TEMPO: Slow   RHYTHM: March or None   COLOR: Organ

Slow and steady

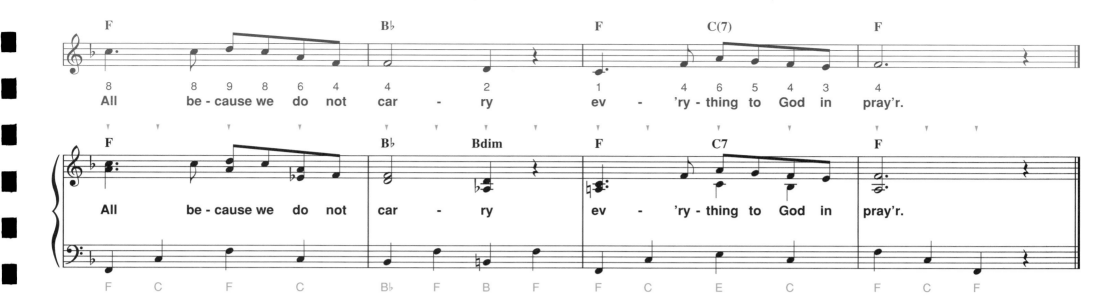

All be - cause we do not car - ry ev - 'ry - thing to God in pray'r.

8 8 9 8 6 4 4 2 1 4 6 5 4 3 4

All be - cause we do not car - ry ev - 'ry - thing to God in pray'r.

F C F C B♭ F B F F C E C F C F

Additional Verses

2. Have we trials and temptations,
Is there trouble anywhere?
We should never be discouraged;
Take it to the Lord in pray'r.
Can we find a friend so faithful,
Who will all our sorrows share?
Jesus knows our ev'ry weakness;
Take it to the Lord in pray'r.

3. Are we weak and heavy laden,
Cumbered with a load of care?
Precious Savior still our refuge;
Take it to the Lord in pray'r.
Do thy friends despise, forsake thee?
Take it to the Lord in pray'r.
In His arms He'll take and shield thee;
Thou wilt find a solace there.

HIS EYE IS ON THE SPARROW

Words by Mrs. C.D. Martin;
Music by Charles H. Gabriel

TEMPO: Slow   RHYTHM: Slow Rock   COLOR: Organ/Flute and Harp

132

Additional Verses

2. "Let not thy heart be troubled," His tender word I hear,
   And resting on His goodness, I lose my doubts and fears.
   Tho' by the path He leadeth, but one step I may see.
   His eye is on the sparrow, and I know He watches me.
   His eye is on the sparrow, and I know He watches me.

3. Whenever I am tempted, whenever clouds arise,
   When song gives place to sighing, when hope within me dies,
   I draw the closer to Him, from care He sets me free.
   His eye is on the sparrow, and I know He watches me.
   His eye is on the sparrow, and I know He watches me.

133

Words by Knowles Shaw; Music by George A. Minor

134

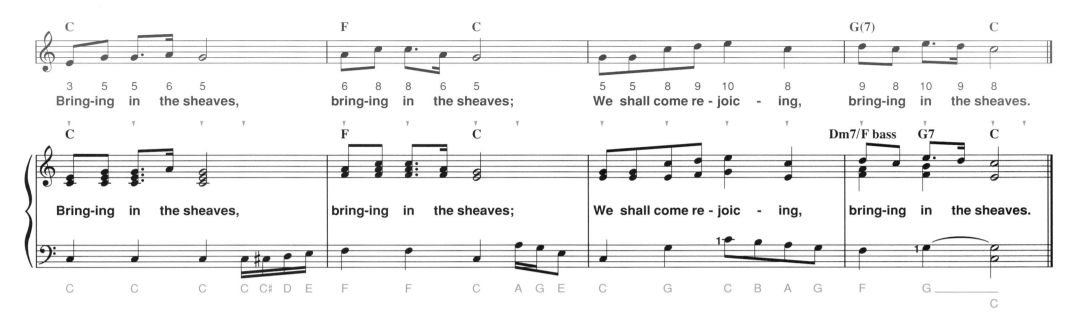

Bring-ing in the sheaves, bring-ing in the sheaves; We shall come re-joic - ing, bring-ing in the sheaves.

Additional Verses

2. Sowing in the sunshine, sowing in the shadows,
Fearing neither clouds nor winter's chilling breeze;
By and by the harvest and the labor ended,
We shall come rejoicing, bringing in the sheaves.
(Repeat Chorus)

3. Going forth with weeping, sowing for the Master,
Tho' the loss sustained our spirit often grieves;
When our weeping's over He will bid us welcome,
We shall come rejoicing, bringing in the sheaves.
(Repeat Chorus)

ROCK OF AGES

Words by Augustus M. Toplady; Music by Thomas Hastings

TEMPO: Moderately slow   RHYTHM: None   COLOR: Organ

Moderately slow and stately

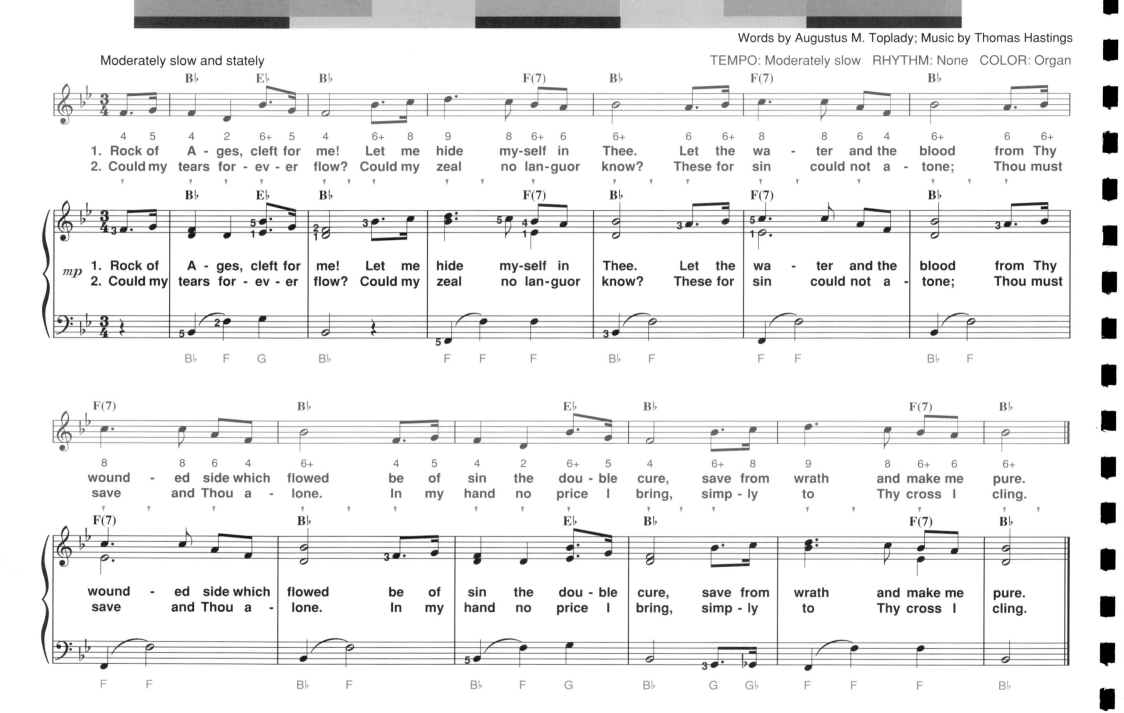

1. Rock of A - ges, cleft for me! Let me hide my-self in Thee. Let the wa - ter and the blood from Thy
2. Could my tears for - ev - er flow? Could my zeal no lan-guor know? These for sin could not a - tone; Thou must

wound - ed side which flowed be of sin the dou - ble cure, save from wrath and make me pure.
save and Thou a - lone. In my hand no price I bring, simp - ly to Thy cross I cling.

Nearer, My God, to Thee

Words by Sarah Fuller Adams; Music by Lowell Mason

TEMPO: Moderate   RHYTHM: None   COLOR: Organ

Additional Verses

2. Tho' like the wanderer,
   The sun gone down,
   Darkness be over me,
   My rest a stone.
   Yet in my dreams I'd be
   Nearer, my God, to Thee,
   Nearer, my God, to Thee,
   Nearer to Thee.

3. There let the way appear,
   Steps unto Heav'n,
   All that Thou sendest me
   In mercy giv'n.
   Angels to beckon me
   Nearer, my God, to Thee, *etc.*

4. Then with my waking thoughts,
   Bright with Thy praise,
   Out of my stony griefs,
   Bethel I'll praise.
   So by my woes to be
   Nearer, my God, to Thee, *etc.*

SECTION EIGHT
Beloved Spirituals

What we now call "spirituals" were originally known as "spiritual songs," to differentiate them from the more formal psalm tunes traditionally used in the English church and in most urban churches in America. Spirituals took several forms: folk hymns, "sorrow songs," hand-clapping "walkarounds," and "call-and-response" songs, during which a line is sung out by the leader and a response is echoed by the rest of the congregation.

Music lovers agree that spirituals are among America's most beautiful religious music. People today tend to think of them as African-American in origin, but in fact there were white spirituals in addition to slave songs. One early witness to their power was Col. Thomas Wentworth Higginson, whose command of a black Union regiment in the Civil War was immortalized in the 1989 film *Glory*. Hearing his enlistees singing spirituals with intense fervor, he saw the music as "not only a source of relaxation but a stimulus to courage and a tie to heaven." Any musical ear cannot fail to discern the burning faith, the deep emotion and the rhythmic vitality of spirituals that make them different from any other kind of music in the world.

Spirituals began to catch the American imagination in the aftermath of the Civil War. In 1871, a group of 11 black students known as the Fisk Jubilee Singers began to perform them on concert tours to raise money for newly founded Fisk University, a college for former slaves in Nashville, Tennessee. Their director, George White, discovered that the more spirituals were put on the program, the bigger the audience. Various soloists can also take credit for making them widely known in recent decades. The great contralto Marian Anderson said that her public always demanded encores of "Deep River" and "Sometimes I Feel Like a Motherless Child." Mahalia Jackson, Paul Robeson, Roland Hayes, Leontyne Price, Jessye Norman and Kathleen Battle have also bestowed on spirituals the prestige their magnificence and uniqueness fully warrant.

Deep River (page 140)
Water has for centuries been an important symbol in the Christian religion and most other religions of the world. Water's purity washes away sin, its cleansing baptizes us into a new life, its healing power soothes the heart, the soul and the body, and its necessity for our physical lives has a parallel in its balm to our spirituality. A river, especially, is a metaphor for faith flowing in us. In this spiritual, a sinner, borne through the slow timeless drift of the "deep river Jordan," not only cleanses himself but escapes finally from the sufferings of life—slavery, hardship, poverty—to find his home in that sweet kingdom where "all the saints above" will entertain him forever.

Go Down, Moses (page 146)
As this spiritual indicates, African-American slaves identified with the captivity of the ancient Israelites in Egypt and how the Lord set them free. In the Book of Exodus, God tells Moses to go to Pharaoh and say, "Thus saith the Lord, 'Let My people go, that they may serve Me.'" The words of "Go Down, Moses" were published at the beginning of the Civil War in an issue of *The National Anti-Slavery Standard*. Soon afterward they appeared with music that had been collected by the Rev. L.C. Lockwood, chaplain of the Contrabands, as those slaves were called who had escaped to the Union lines at Fort Monroe, Virginia. The song also provides an analogy to Harriet Tubman, an escaped slave who returned repeatedly to the South to guide others to freedom by way of the Underground Railway.

Swing Low, Sweet Chariot (page 142)
When the Lord looked with favor on one of His children of whom He was especially fond, He sent a magnificent chariot to bring the beloved one to His side, as in the Second Book of Kings: "And behold, there appeared a chariot of fire, and horses of fire, and Elijah went up by a whirlwind into heaven." What better way to go "home" to one's final resting place "over Jordan." Not only does the Bible give indication of the chariot as a vehicle most mighty and enviable, but painters, particularly in Renaissance times, pictured the inhabitants of Heaven as being transported in magnificent conveyances that seemed to float on the clouds themselves.

Take My Hand, Precious Lord (page 144)
While at a revival meeting in St. Louis in 1932, composer and preacher Thomas A. Dorsey received word that his wife had died in childbirth. He rushed back to his Chicago home only to find that his newborn child had also succumbed just a day later. Prostrate with grief, he began to doubt his faith. "But I could not throw God out of my life," he reflected. One evening after he had attended an inspirational meeting, as he lay sleepless, he kept hearing like a chant the words "take my hand, take my hand. . . ." The effect on him, he said, was "almost like drops of water dripping from the crevice of a rock into a deep calm pool." The song wrung from such sorrow has proved to be a source of strength to countless others, and it triumphantly revivified his own flagging faith as well.

Were You There (When They Crucified My Lord)? (page 139)
According to George Pullen Jackson, an authority on hymns and spirituals, "Were You There?" had been sung, chiefly among black congregations, for several generations before it was finally transcribed and published in a collection of *Old Plantation Hymns* in 1899. Whether it was originally a black or a white spiritual cannot be determined, though there is at least one version that developed in a white region of Tennessee. As a dramatization of the Crucifixion, the song has no equal—a superbly moving and simple reenactment of one of the most momentous events in the history of the world.

When the Saints Go Marching In (page 143)
Probably the most famous Dixieland jazz tune of all time, "When the Saints Go Marching In" apparently originated in the Bahamas, based on an earlier revival tune called "When the Saints March In for Crowning." New Orleans street bands popularized it as a funeral march. Hired brass bands would accompany the coffin to the cemetery, playing at the outset with dignity and muffled drums, but changing to an accelerated tempo and a considerably heightened volume as the funeral party returned through the streets. Jazz trumpeter Louis Armstrong made a recording in 1938 that has influenced nearly every subsequent performance, and Bunk Johnson's version is equally renowned.

Were You There

(When They Crucified My Lord)?

Traditional

Continue similarly . . .
2. Were you there when they nailed Him to the cross? . . .
3. Were you there when they laid Him in the tomb? . . .
4. Were you there when He rose up from the grave? . . .

DEEP RIVER

Traditional

TEMPO: Moderately slow   RHYTHM: None   COLOR: Organ or Strings

Moderately slow

140

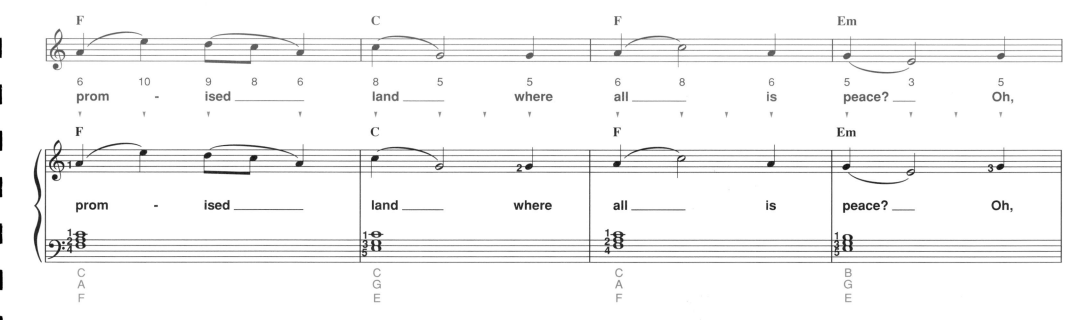

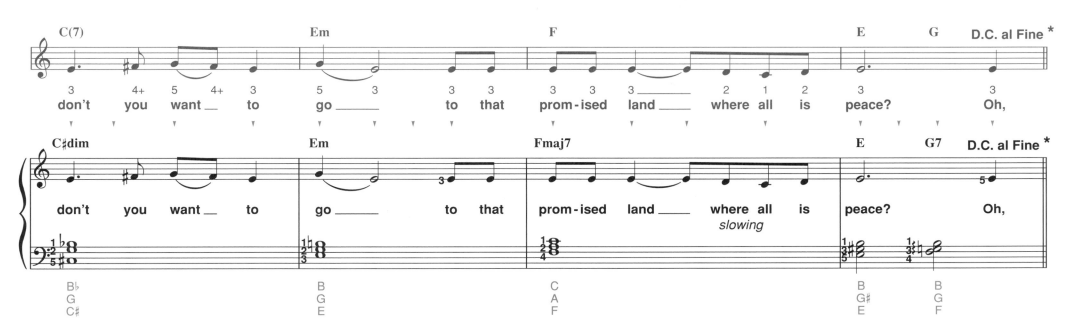

*Repeat from the beginning through to the word "Fine".

SWING LOW, SWEET CHARIOT

Traditional

TEMPO: Slow   RHYTHM: None   COLOR: Organ

When the Saints Go Marching In

Traditional

Moderately, with a beat

TEMPO: Moderate   RHYTHM: Swing   COLOR: Brass Ensemble or Harpsichord

Continue similarly
2. And when the revelation comes . . .
3. And when they crown Him King of Kings . . .
4. And when the sun begins to shine . . .
5. Oh, when the saints go marching in . . .

143

Take My Hand, Precious Lord

Words and Music by
the Rev. Thomas A. Dorsey

TEMPO: Slow   RHYTHM: None   COLOR: Organ or Synth Reed

144

*Repeat from the beginning to the word "Fine".

GO DOWN, MOSES

Traditional

TEMPO: Slow   RHYTHM: None   COLOR: Organ

Additional Verses

2. Thus saith the Lord, bold Moses said,
Let my people go!
If not I'll smite your first-born dead,
Let my people go!
(Repeat Chorus)

3. No more shall they in bondage toil,
Let my people go!
Let them come out with Egypt's spoil,
Let my people go!
(Repeat Chorus)

4. Oh, Moses, the cloud shall cleave the way,
Let my people go!
A fire by night, a shade by day,
Let my people go!
(Repeat Chorus)

5. Your foes shall not before you stand,
Let my people go!
And you'll possess fair Canaan's land
Let my people go!
(Repeat Chorus)

146

SECTION NINE
Sunday School Memories

The Bible Tells Me So (page 148)

The producer of the television show that starred Dale Evans and her husband, Roy Rogers, came to her one day in 1955 while they were taping a segment. He told her that the script called for a little girl to sing, and he could not find a song that was suitable. Could she compose something? Quickly? "A Sunday school type of song," he suggested. Dale disappeared into her dressing room and prayed for inspiration. Almost immediately the line "Now abideth these three: faith, hope and charity" came to her, and from then on the rest "simply tumbled forth." She dashed it off, sang it over, taught it to the petite songstress, and into the show it went. "The Bible Tells Me So" became a Hit Parade favorite for weeks and soon found its way into Roy Rogers' hundreds of performances.

Brighten the Corner Where You Are (page 152)

Prevented from fulfilling her desire to be a Chautauqua evangelist by the necessity of caring for her invalid father, Ina Duley Ogdon instead dedicated herself to making his life more cheerful and comfortable. One of her gifts to him was a bit of verse that exemplified her brisk and generous philosophy. Charles Gabriel, generous friend of many gospel poets, set her stanzas to music as perky and memorable as her lyrics, and "Brighten the Corner Where You Are" was introduced in 1912 by the ubiquitous revivalist and friend of Billy Sunday, Homer Rodeheaver.

I Love to Tell the Story (page 154)

William G. Fischer, of the famous Philadelphia piano-manufacturing family, loved to lift his hearty, mellow baritone in song at revival meetings. In the 1860s, he discovered a long poem on the life of Jesus by English author Arabella Katherine Hankey, a banker's daughter whose ill health required her to spend long hours in bed. Writing was a pleasant way of spending such time, and her strong religious zeal was a constant inspiration to her thought. Fischer, who often wrote gospel music, supplied an easy, appealing tune for "I Love to Tell the Story," a short section of Miss Hankey's original work, which had been published in 1866 with royalties donated entirely to charity. The Hankey-Fischer segment appeared in 1869 in *Joyful Songs*. Mercantile genius and gospel enthusiast John Wanamaker honored Fischer at a huge Sunday school convention in Philadelphia shortly before the latter's death. The music? "I Love to Tell the Story."

Jacob's Ladder (page 158)

"Jacob's Ladder," thought to be a white spiritual, is based on Jacob's dream as told in Genesis 28—how at sunset when he had arranged the desert stones to be his pillows and had fallen asleep, he saw "a ladder set up on the earth, and the top of it reached to heaven: and behold there were angels of God ascending and descending it. And behold, the Lord stood above it and said, 'I am the Lord God of Abraham thy father, and the God of Isaac.'" Then the Lord promises to give Jacob and his descendants the land on which he is lying, and to watch over him and bring him back to the land of Canaan. When he awoke, Jacob was awestruck by the dream and named the place Bethel ("House of God"), ever after a sacred place for the ancient Hebrews. (See also "Nearer, My God, to Thee," page 121.)

Jesus Loves the Little Children (page 156)

Several of George F. Root's songs, such as "Just Before the Battle, Mother" and "Battle Cry of Freedom," were written during the Civil War, but his musical imagination covered a wide field. From singing boy soprano in a Boston church to a career with his brother in a Chicago music-publishing house, he always maintained a strong interest in religious music. A friend of his, the Chicago preacher C.H. Woolston, wrote the words of "Jesus Loves the Little Children" especially for Root's stirring if somewhat martial "Tramp! Tramp! Tramp!" song from the war-torn days of 1863. A century later, Ray Stevens used its refrain as the introduction to his hit song "Everything Is Beautiful" (see page 52).

Jesus Wants Me for a Sunbeam (page 159)

Nellie Talbot thought she had run out of lessons for the Sunday school class that she had been teaching in a little Missouri church—until she stopped to chide herself for lack of imagination. "How can you say there's nothing to teach about when you have the sun and the sky and the trees and the flowers!" So she set to work on the sun (in the form of a sunbeam) and enjoyed her own lesson so much that she wrote it down in verse. With gospel hymnist E.O. Excell's "excellent" music, her inspirational song remains one of today's favorites.

Oh Happy Day (page 150)

One of the hardest-working preachers in London, despite severe health problems, Philip Doddridge wrote his many hymns for the use of his congregation and often did not bother to print them. In those days, hymns were read out line by line and simply echoed or sung by those participating. His "Oh Happy Day," a paraphrase of some verses from Psalm 56, was published—but only, alas, after he had died in Lisbon of consumption in 1751.

His text came to the attention of the English organist and musicologist Edward Rimbault, who composed a celebratory setting a century later. The stirring music so captivated Prince Albert that the latter insisted the hymn be played and sung at the confirmations of his and Queen Victoria's several children.

Onward, Christian Soldiers (page 160)

The stirring music of "Onward, Christian Soldiers" is the product of Sir Arthur Sullivan, composer not only of the famous "Lost Chord" but of all the operettas, such as *H.M.S. Pinafore* and *The Mikado*, that he created with his witty playwright associate, W.S. Gilbert. The words for "Onward, Christian Soldiers" came not from the irreverent Gilbert but from an English divine, Sabine Baring-Gould, who one evening in 1865 was trying to write something for the children of his parish to sing for the Whitsunday procession. "I just sat up all night," he said later, "until I thought of something." Winston Churchill picked that "something" to be part of the ceremonies at the signing of the Atlantic Charter on board the *Prince of Wales* on August 10, 1941, because, he said, "I felt we were serving a cause for the sake of which a trumpet has sounded on high!" President Franklin D. Roosevelt was among those whose voices, along with Churchill's, were raised in song on that historic occasion.

The Bible Tells Me So

Words and Music by Dale Evans

OH HAPPY DAY

Words by Philip Doddridge; Music by E.F. Rimbault

TEMPO: Moderate   RHYTHM: Waltz or None   COLOR: Organ

Additional Verses

2. Oh happy bond that seals my vows
    To Him who merits all my love!
    Let cheerful anthems fill His house,
    While to that sacred shrine I move.
    (Repeat Chorus)

3. 'Tis done, the great transaction's done;
    I am my Lord's, and He is mine.
    He drew me, and I followed on,
    Charmed to confess the voice divine.
    (Repeat Chorus)

4. Now rest my long divided heart;
    Fixed on this blissful center rest.
    Nor ever from my Lord depart,
    With Him of ev'ry good possessed.
    (Repeat Chorus)

Brighten the Corner Where You Are

Words by Ina Duley Ogdon; Music by Charles M. Gabriel

TEMPO: Moderate   RHYTHM: Big Band or Swing   COLOR: Kalimba, Jazz Guitar or Clarinet

Additional Verses

2. Just above are clouded skies that you may help to clear,
   Let not narrow self your way debar;
   Though into one heart alone may fall your song of cheer,
   Brighten the corner where you are.
   (Repeat Chorus)

3. Here for all your talent you may surely find a need,
   Here reflect the bright and morning star;
   Even from your humble hand the bread of life may feed,
   Brighten the corner where you are.
   (Repeat Chorus)

154

Additional Verses

2. I love to tell the story,
   More wonderful it seems
   Than all the golden fancies
   Of all our golden dreams.
   I love to tell the story,
   It did so much for me;
   And that is just the reason
   I tell it now to thee.
   (Repeat Chorus)

3. I love to tell the story
   'Tis pleasant to repeat,
   What seems each time I tell it
   More wonderfully sweet.
   I love to tell the story,
   For some have never heard
   The message of salvation
   From God's own holy word.
   (Repeat Chorus)

4. I love to tell the story,
   For those who know it best
   Seem hungering and thirsting
   To hear it like the rest.
   And when in scenes of glory
   I sing the new, new song,
   'Twill be the old, old story
   That I have loved so long.
   (Repeat Chorus)

Words by C.H. Woolston;
Music by George F. Root

TEMPO: Moderate   RHYTHM: March or None   COLOR: Organ or Flute

Additional Verses

2. Jesus is the Shepherd true,
   And He'll always stand by you,
   For He loves the children of the world;
   He's a Savior great and strong,
   And He'll shield you from the wrong,
   For He loves the little children of the world.
   (Repeat Chorus)

3. I am coming, Lord, to Thee,
   And Thy soldier I will be,
   For He loves the little children of the world;
   And His cross I'll always bear,
   And for Him I'll do and dare,
   For He loves the little children of the world.
   (Repeat Chorus)

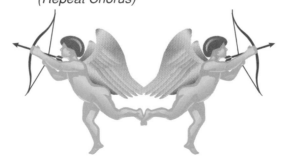

Jacob's Ladder

Traditional

TEMPO: Slow   RHYTHM: None   COLOR: Synth Strings

Slowly

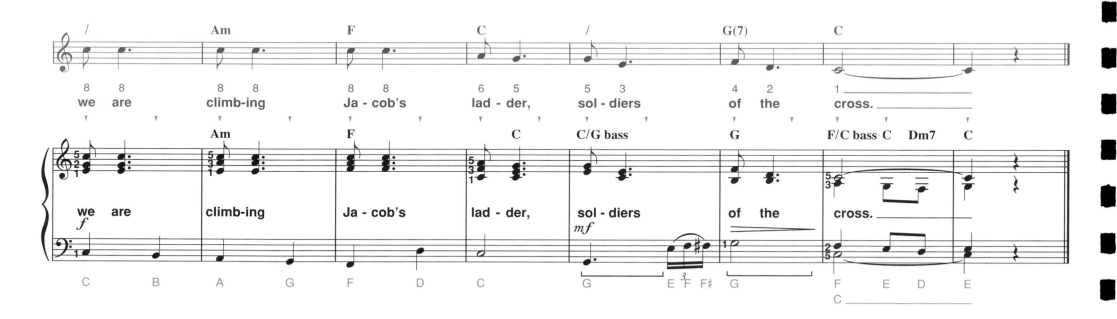

Additional Verses

2. Ev'ry round goes higher, higher,
   Ev'ry round goes higher, higher,
   Ev'ry round goes higher, higher,
   Soldiers of the cross.

Continue similarly:

3. Sinners, do you love my Jesus?...

4. If you love Him, why not serve Him?...

5. We are climbing higher, higher...

6. We are climbing Jacob's ladder...

158

Jesus Wants Me for a Sunbeam

Words by Nellie Talbor; Music by E.O. Excell

Slowly in 2 (each ♪. = 1 beat)

TEMPO: Moderately fast   RHYTHM: None   COLOR: Organ or Celeste/Vibraphone

Onward, Christian Soldiers

Words by Sabine Baring-Gould;
Music by Sir Arthur Sullivan

TEMPO: Moderate   RHYTHM: March or None   COLOR: Organ

Additional Verses

2. Like a mighty army moves the Church of God;
   Brothers, we are treading where the saints have trod.
   We are not divided, all one body we,
   One in hope and doctrine, one in charity.
   (Repeat Chorus)

3. Onward, then, ye people, join our happy throng,
   Blend with ours your voices in the triumph song;
   Glory, laud and honor unto Christ the King,
   This through countless ages, men and angels sing:
   (Repeat Chorus)

Let a Smile Be Your Umbrella (page 166)
One of the most beloved songwriters in popular music was Sammy Fain, whose brilliant melodies were first set off, with equal brilliance, by the lyrics of Irving Kahal. "Let a Smile Be Your Umbrella" was one of the early successes of Fain and Kahal, written in 1927 (with help on the words from Francis Wheeler) and first sung in vaudeville by Fain and his vocal-duet partner, Artie Dunn. Kahal's death in 1942 led to other successful partnerships with Wheeler, Lew Brown and especially Paul Francis Webster in the '50s. Fain and Webster produced such classics as "April Love" and the two Oscar-winners "Secret Love," which Doris Day introduced in the film *Calamity Jane*, and "Love Is a Many-Splendored Thing," a No.1 hit by The Four Aces from the film of the same name.

Make Someone Happy (page 163)
The best song from the 1960 Broadway musical *Do Re Mi* was "Make Someone Happy," which was sung in the show by John Reardon and Nancy Dussault. The talented team that produced the tune consisted of composer Jule Styne and lyricists Betty Comden and Adolph Green. The title, however, proved ironic: the show never earned enough "do-re-mi" to be financially profitable. The message of this song was not concerned with financial gain, of course, but with simple pleasure—its verses based on the old Sunday school proverb, "In order to be happy you must first make others happy." Which the song has been doing for several decades.

On the Sunny Side of the Street (page 172)
When young writer Dorothy Fields, daughter of comic Lew Fields (of Weber and Fields), met the similarly young composer Jimmy McHugh in 1928, it was a happy turning point for both of them. Their first collaboration was a tremendously successful revue, *Blackbirds of 1928*. A year later they worked together again on *Lew Leslie's International Revue*, two songs from which have been standards ever since. "Exactly Like You" was a favorite of orchestra leader Jimmy Lunceford, and "On the Sunny Side of the Street" was introduced in the show by Gertrude Lawrence—later to create the role of Anna in *The King and I*—and leading man Harry Richman.

One Little Candle (page 178)
The inspiration for this song is the motto of the Christopher Society: "It is better to light one candle than to curse the darkness." The lyrics by J. Maloy Roach and George Mysels also are reminiscent of Portia's speech in Shakespeare's *The Merchant of Venice*, which likens the light of a candle to a good deed "in a naughty world." Roach and Mysels, both of whom had lit musical candles of their own for the world's good by entertaining troops at military bases during World War II, wrote their song in 1951. It became a big success the next year, thanks to Perry Como's hit recording.

Put On a Happy Face (page 170)
Long ago there lived a man so surpassingly ugly that his neighbors persuaded him to wear a mask with a smile on it. He wore the mask for so many years that when it accidentally broke, the neighbors didn't notice, because by then his real face had come to resemble the smiling mask. Such is the message of this song, written by Lee Adams and Charles Strouse in 1960 for their irreverent Broadway debut, *Bye Bye Birdie*, which lampooned Elvis Presley. Bubbling with new songs and new stars (among them Dick Van Dyke and Chita Rivera), it won a Tony for Best Musical.

Smile (page 168)
"Smile" was written by Charlie Chaplin in 1936 for perhaps his finest film, *Modern Times*. He was its star, scenarist, writer, stunt man and musical director. In his acting role as a corporate lamb thrown to the gray-flanneled wolves of modern commerce, his only weapon was a winsome little smile, echoed throughout by this charming melody. In 1954, long after the movie had won a wide public, two lyricists, John Turner and Geoffrey Parsons, extracted the melody from the background score and put words to it. The resulting song was recorded in a number of fine performances, among them those by Tony Bennett and Nat "King" Cole.

Smiles (page 176)
What America needed in 1917 was a nice, cheerful song that did not mention the war, and that is exactly what J. Will Callahan and Lee S. Roberts decided to write. Roberts, associated with a player-piano company, was attending a music dealers' convention in Chicago when he heard a keynote speech that emphasized the importance of a smile. Then and there he dashed off a perky tune on the back of a cigarette package and sent it to his friend Callahan, who responded with a cute lyric in no time. When the two couldn't find a publisher, they issued it themselves and shared the profits of two million copies sold.

What a Wonderful World (page 180)
"Louis really loved this tune," clarinetist Joe Muranyi once said, speaking of "What a Wonderful World" and trumpeter Louis Armstrong. "He seemed to identify with it on a lot of levels." In the late '60s, everyone was looking for respite from domestic and international tensions—assassinations, race riots, the war in Vietnam. So songwriters George David Weiss and Bob Thiele decided to put their accent on the positive and make a beautiful, tender song. In 1967, Armstrong's subdued version became his last major hit. Sixteen years after his death, in 1987, "What a Wonderful World" was used in the film *Good Morning, Vietnam*, and the same Armstrong recording swooped back up the charts as part of the soundtrack album.

When You're Smiling (the Whole World Smiles with You) (page 174)
"When You're Smiling," another Louis Armstrong specialty, dates from 1928. It's the endearing product of collaborators Larry Shay, Joe Goodwin and Mark Fisher, who were still basking in the success of their "Everywhere You Go" from the previous year. Armstrong had just begun recording with his new jazz band, and their "When You're Smiling" was an immediate hit and made the song a standard. Frank Sinatra reprised it in the 1952 film *Meet Danny Wilson*, in which he plays a singer entangled with criminal elements.

Make Someone Happy

Words by Betty Comden
and Adolph Green;
Music by Jule Styne

Moderate swing

TEMPO: Moderate   RHYTHM: Swing   COLOR: (Synth) Reeds or Jazz Organ

Words by Irving Kahal
and Francis Wheeler;
Music by Sammy Fain

166

Smîle

Words by John Turner and Geoffrey Parsons; Music by Charlie Chaplin

TEMPO: Moderate   RHYTHM: Swing   COLOR: Strings

PUT ON A HAPPY FACE

Words by Lee Adams; Music by Charles Strouse

On the Sunny Side of the Street

Words by Dorothy Fields; Music by Jimmy McHugh

WHEN YOU'RE SMILING
(the Whole World Smiles with You)

Words and Music by Mark Fisher, Joe Goodwin and Larry Shay

TEMPO: Moderate   RHYTHM: Swing   COLOR: Clarinet or Jazz Organ

Moderate swing tempo

When you're smil - ing, when you're smil - ing, the whole world

When you're smil - ing, when you're smil - ing, the whole world

smiles with you. When you're laugh - ing, when you're laugh - ing,

smiles with you. When you're laugh - ing, when you're laugh - ing,

the sun comes shin - ing thru. But when you're

the sun comes shin - ing thru. But when you're

174

Words by J. Will Callahan; Music by Lee S. Roberts

TEMPO: Moderately bright   RHYTHM: Swing   COLOR: Flute, Strings, Honky-tonk Piano

One Little Candle

Words and Music by J. Maloy Roach and George Mysels

What a Wonderful World

Words and Music by Bob Thiele and George David Weiss

TEMPO: Slow   RHYTHM: Slow Rock   COLOR: Trumpet or Strings

Bless the Beasts and Children (page 188)

The most successful part of the fine score that Barry DeVorzon and Perry Botkin, Jr., wrote for Stanley Kramer's 1971 film *Bless the Beasts and Children* was the title song. In addition to giving hit singles to The Carpenters the next year and to the DeVorzon-Botkin duo in 1977, it was nominated for an Academy Award. (It lost to the "Theme Music from *Shaft*.") The movie dealt with a group of boys who are intent on saving a herd of buffalo from destruction. The background music produced another hit song, extracted to accompany the television soap opera *The Young and the Restless*, and also as a theme for the young Romanian Olympic gymnast Nadia Comaneci. (The title of the melody touches all bases: "Nadia's Theme from *The Young and the Restless*.") The Carpenters' recording of "Bless the Beasts and Children" charted for ten weeks in 1971, the year after they had won their Grammy as Best New Artist and the season they became hosts of their first television show, *Make Your Own Kind of Music*.

Bless This House (page 190)

Poet Helen Taylor and composer May Brahe, two English friends, combined their talents in 1927 on this appealing song, calling it "Bless the House." It caught the ear of the superb Irish tenor John McCormack, whose canny instincts told him the title should be changed to "Bless *This* House." (He suggested a few similarly adroit changes in the lyrics as well.) With his alterations, the song, frequently and ravishingly performed by its champion, became popular in England. McCormack also programmed it often on his radio performances in the United States. When it was chosen as the closing theme for the distinguished 1940s radio program *The Prudential Family Hour*, "Bless This House" attained the status of a true classic.

Blest Be the Tie That Binds (page 200)

John Fawcett, an impoverished young clergyman in a small but hospitable village in the northeast of England, earned such a scanty salary that he simply could not maintain his growing family. So when he received an offer from a wealthier parish in London in 1772, he decided to accept the invitation. Household all packed and ready, he made the fatal mistake of preaching one last sermon to his sorrowing congregation. Sentiment reigned increasingly as the sermon went on, and his audience's ready tears and lamenting sighs so undid him that he unpacked his goods and remained where he was. Perhaps by way of commemoration of the event, Fawcett jotted down the verses we know as "Blest Be the Tie That Binds," which in a gentle setting by Swiss composer Hans Georg Nägeli (1773–1836), later became a favorite of congregations everywhere.

Let There Be Peace on Earth (page 196)

Seymour "Sy" Miller, a New York City vaudeville, radio and TV composer, wrote a number of songs with his actress wife, Jill Jackson, chief among them "Let There Be Peace on Earth," also known as "Let It Begin with Me." The song was popularized by its use in the "Crusade for Peace" program, for which Miller won the Freedoms Foundation George Washington Honor Medal and the Brotherhood Award in 1958. It also was included in a U.S. Information Agency documentary about Japan. Both Miller and his wife became well-known speakers throughout the country on behalf of peace.

The Lord's Prayer (page 184)

Albert Hay Malotte, born in 1895 in Philadelphia and educated there, found himself as a young man in the employ of the Walt Disney Studios, where he composed the score for *Ferdinand the Bull*. He also turned his hand to a number of songs, both secular and religious, including "The Lord's Prayer." When he had finished his manuscript of the sacred prayer, he sent it to the prominent music publisher G. Schirmer. Someone at the firm, which had just issued another setting of "The Lord's Prayer," was supposed to send a rejection letter to Malotte, but before it got into the mail, Malotte's version was performed on the radio in Pittsburgh by baritone John Charles Thomas. As a result, music stores received so many requests for the sheet music that the publisher rescued Malotte's manuscript from the "Out" box and changed the letter to one of acceptance. "The Lord's Prayer" was published in 1935 and became one of the biggest sellers Schirmer ever had. Not surprisingly, it was dedicated to Thomas and was frequently sung by him thereafter. Its text is, of course, that uttered by Jesus in His Sermon on the Mount as an example of how to pray (Matthew 6:9–13).

My Prayer for Today (page 193)

Hoagy Carmichael, composer of such evergreens as "Star Dust" and "Georgia on My Mind," had already had several successful collaborations with his sister-in-law, the radio and film author Helen Stearns, prior to 1959, the year they accidentally combined to write "My Prayer for Today." Her lyric was composed first, at the behest of a New York publisher, but as she related, "I was having trouble with a melody for it. Mine all sounded a bit manufactured." One afternoon brother-in-law Hoagy noticed her poem on the piano and said, "I like this; can I take a crack at it?" He came up with "this lilting little tune," which pleased her so much that she later included "My Prayer for Today" in a collection of Carmichael's songs for children, where it has added another age group to the wide audience that it enjoys today.

The Lord's Prayer

Music by Albert Hay Malotte

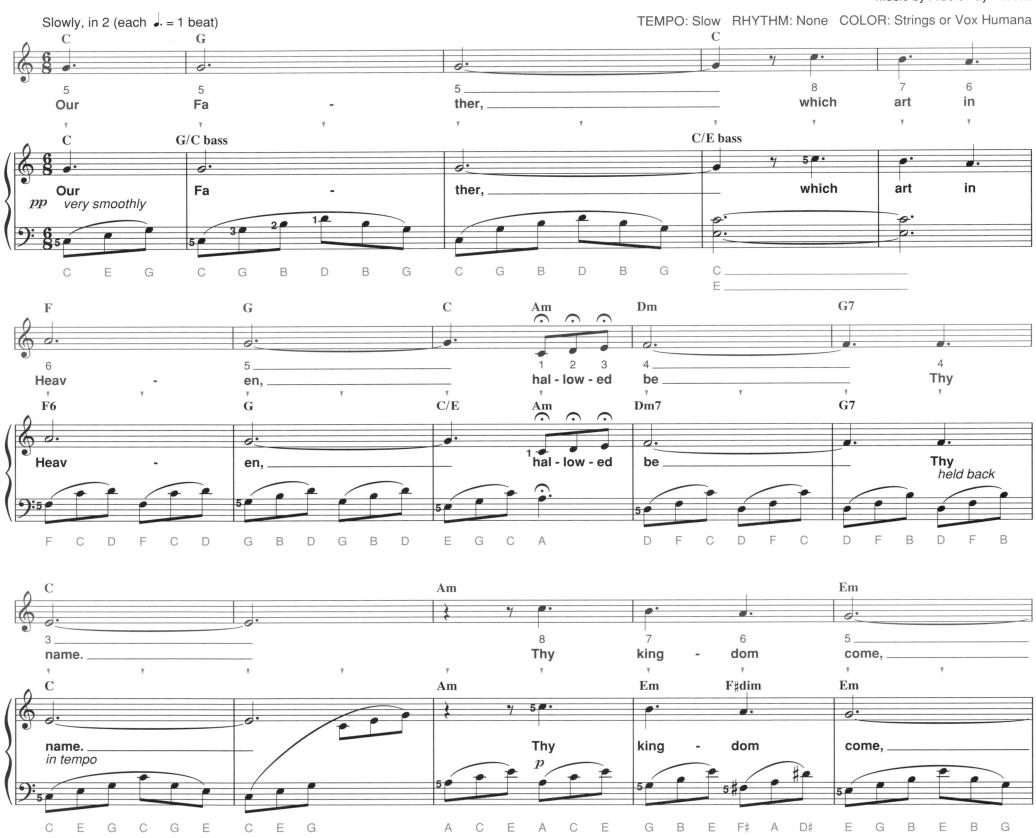

*The tempo stays the same, but now each measure gets three slow beats instead of two

**Same tempo, but four slow beats per measure.

Words by Helen Taylor;
Music by May H. Brahe

MY PRAYER FOR TODAY

Words by Helen Stearns;
Music by Hoagy Carmichael

TEMPO: Moderate   RHYTHM: Waltz   COLOR: Piano (sustain on), Synth Reed

193

Let There Be Peace on Earth

Words and Music by
Jill Jackson and Sy Miller

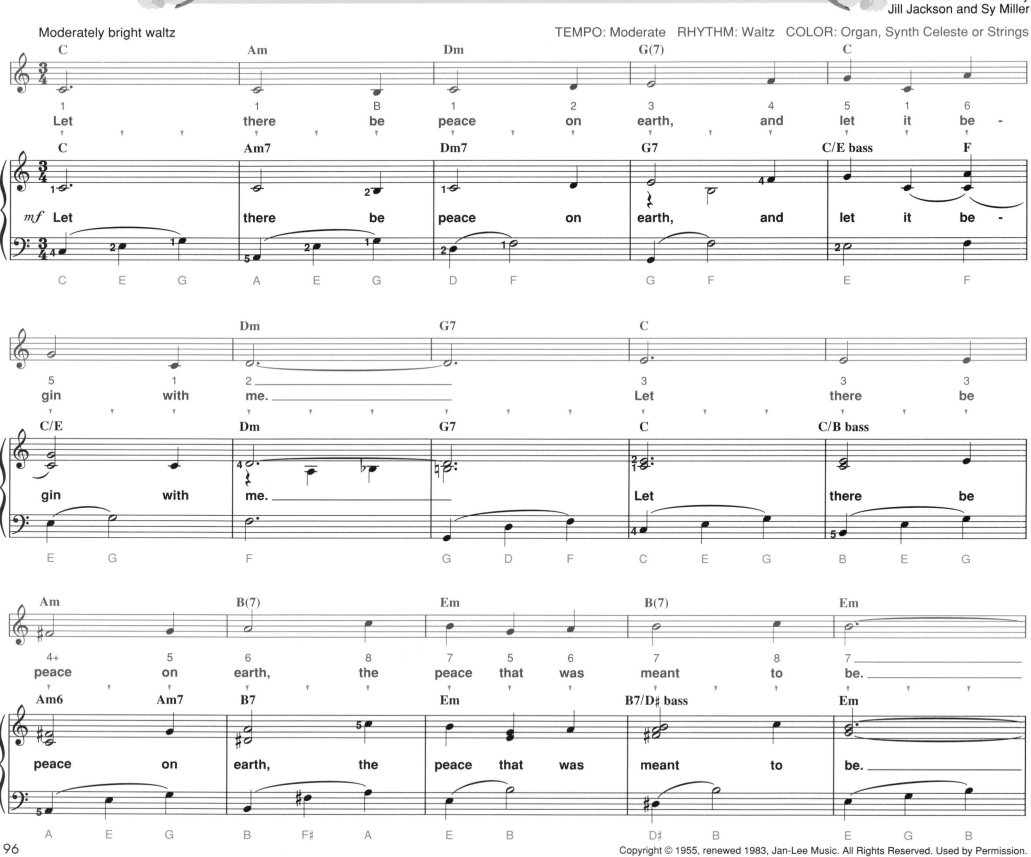

196

Blest Be the Tie That Binds

Words by John Fawcett; Music by Hans Georg Nägeli

TEMPO: Moderate   RHYTHM: None   COLOR: Flute or Organ

Additional Verses

2. Before our Father's throne
   We pour our ardent prayers.
   Our fears, our hopes, our aims are one,
   Our comforts and our cares.

3. We share our mutual woes,
   Our mutual burdens bear,
   And often for each other flows
   The sympathizing tear.

4. When we asunder part
   It gives us inward pain.
   But we shall still be joined in heart
   And hope to meet again.

200

SECTION TWELVE
Beyond the Sunset/Songs for the Twilight Hours

Abide with Me (page 205)

A Scottish man of the cloth, Henry Francis Lyte (1793–1847), wrote this lovely hymn when he was only 27, following close upon his visit to a dying friend who kept repeating the phrase "Abide with me." Lyte gave a copy of his verses to the patient's brother but probably did not publish them until he was about to retire from the rigors of his parish—thus the story that he had felt his own end approaching and was inspired to jot them down then, 27 years later. Lyte was so devoted to his congregation in the English fishing village of Brixham that, it was said, no boat left the harbor without his blessing. Ironically, he had intended to become a doctor, but his own health was always frail, and his ministry undermined it further. He died of tuberculosis in the south of France shortly after his early retirement. The tune to which Lyte's most famous hymn is sung came from the pen of William H. Monk (1823–89), English organist and editor of the most famous of Anglican hymnals, *Hymns Ancient and Modern*. His wife later said he had written it outdoors as they watched the setting sun together.

Beautiful Isle of Somewhere (page 212)

Jessie Brown, who was born in Ohio shortly before the Civil War and died shortly after World War I, married John E. Pounds, a Disciples of Christ minister, and became a prolific writer of inspirational books, musical texts and hymns. She was only 15 when she offered her first verses to the editor of a religious magazine. "Beautiful Isle of Somewhere," probably her best-loved work, was set to music by the gospel composer John S. Fearis and became a favorite song of President William McKinley, at whose funeral it was sung.

Beyond the Sunset (page 214)

The husband-and-wife evangelist songwriters of Virgil and Blanche Kerr Brock were staying in the guest house of gospel composer, singer and publisher Homer Rodeheaver on the shore of Winona Lake in Indiana. As they admired the extraordinary sunset, devotional thoughts came to them: What lies beyond the sunset? What will Heaven be like when we have finished our work here on earth? Their resulting song, "Beyond the Sunset," with words by Virgil and music by Blanche, was published in 1936. It is likely that the melody was adapted from a Scandinavian tune familiar to Swedish immigrants to the Midwest, where both were born.

Blessed Assurance (page 210)

Fanny Jane Crosby, though blind from infancy, began to write poetry as a young girl and hymn-texts at the instigation of composer William Bradbury when she was in her early forties. So prolific was she that at the end of her long life (she died in 1915 at age 95) she had produced about 8,000 songs of praise, sometimes as many as seven a day. For her friend and composer W.H. Doane, she dashed off the words of "Safe in the Arms of Jesus" in about 15 minutes. And in 1873 for another close friend, Mrs. Joseph F. Knapp, wife of the president of Metropolitan Life Insurance Company and with him co-supervisor of two Brooklyn Sunday schools, "Aunt Fanny" produced

"Blessed Assurance" to fit a tune Mrs. Knapp had composed. When Mrs. Knapp first played the melody a few times for her friend, she asked Fanny what the music "said" to her. The hymnist replied, without batting an eye, "Blessed assurance, Jesus is mine." With that ease of understanding between the two women, the song was soon finished.

In the Sweet By and By (page 206)

J.P. Webster, visiting a drugstore in Elkhorn, Wisconsin, operated by his friend Sanford Fillmore Bennett, admitted that he was feeling a bit depressed, but waved away Bennett's solicitude by saying, "It's no matter; it'll be all right by and by." The simple phrase struck a spark in Bennett's imagination, and he began jotting down some verses on the spot. As he wrote, he passed them to Webster, who apparently had a violin with him and who improvised a melody then and there. In less than an hour, they had finished "In the Sweet By and By," and it was published a few years later in their 1867 collection of songs and hymns, *The Signet Ring*.

It Is Well with My Soul (page 208)

Horatio Gates Spafford created beauty out of tragedy. The considerable property losses he sustained in the Chicago Fire of 1871 were nothing compared to the loss of his four daughters, who perished in the collision of two ships at sea a few years later. As Spafford rushed to rejoin his wife, who survived the disaster, and sailed past the site of the sinking near Cardiff, Wales, he plumbed deeply into his faith to pen the words of "It Is Well with My Soul." His friend, Philip P. Bliss, heard the news and composed music for Spafford's verses in tribute. Bliss, a very successful composer and singing evangelist, himself fell victim to a tragic accident. He was on a train with his wife, Lucy, on New Year's Eve, 1876, when a bridge over which they were passing near Ashtabula, Ohio, collapsed. He crawled from the wreckage but went back to rescue his Lucy, and both perished.

Just a Closer Walk with Thee (page 202)

With its true origins lost in the mists of time, "Just a Closer Walk with Thee" probably came into being during the Southern revivalist crusades at the turn of the 20th century. Its greatest popularity still lies in its use by New Orleans Dixieland "funeral bands," which accompany mourning cortèges through the city streets. In 1950, country star Red Foley recorded the chromatic, blues-accented tune and turned it into a million-seller.

Precious Memories (page 204)

J.B.F. Wright wrote "Precious Memories" out of his own poignant reminiscences of a Tennessee childhood full of a loving home and reverent parents—and what he called "unseen angels." Untutored in music, Wright relied on inspiration rather than polished technique to create his songs: "When words come spontaneously flowing into place, when I feel the divine urge," as he put it. "Precious Memories" was published in 1925. Tennessee Ernie Ford, who revived interest in it with his popular 1959 recording, once termed it "a kind of Southern/Western spiritual."

201

Just a Closer Walk with Thee

Traditional

Moderately fast

TEMPO: Moderate   RHYTHM: Country or Slow Rock I   COLOR: Jazz Guitar

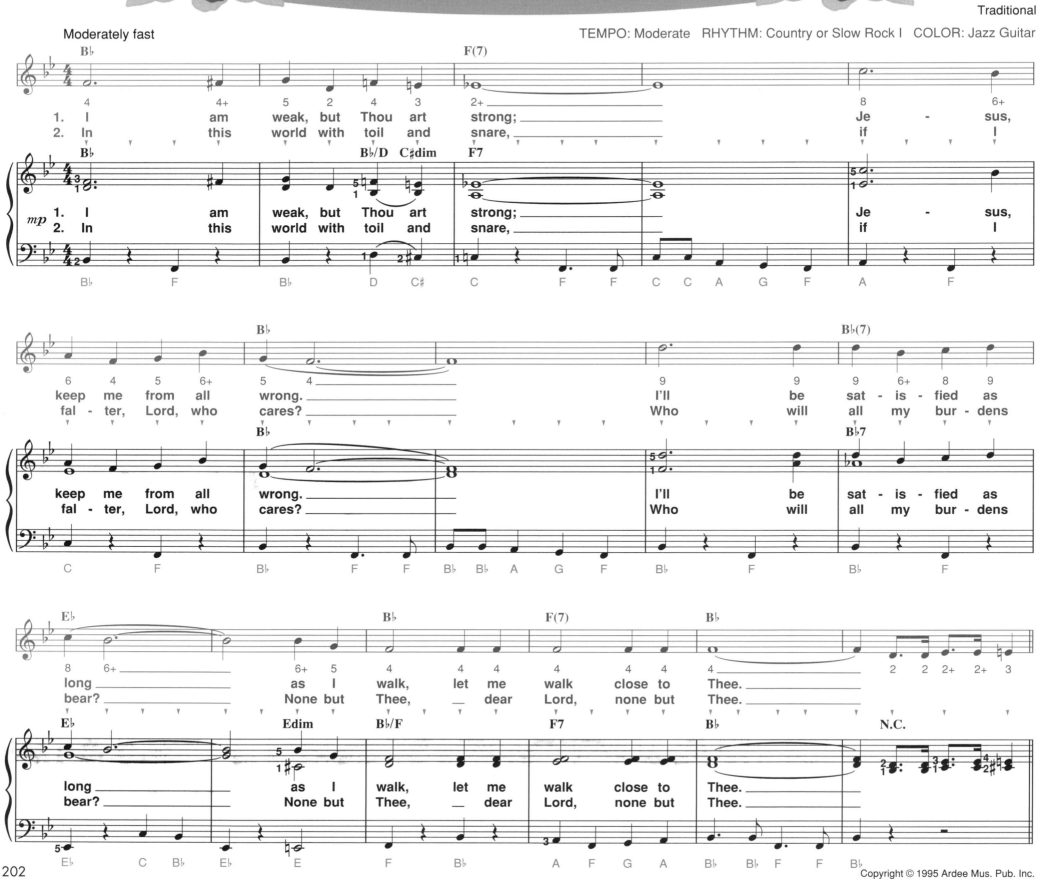

Precious Memories

Words and Music by
J.B.F. Wright

TEMPO: Moderate RHYTHM: None* COLOR: (Reed) organ

*Play each chord where its symbol appears. A "/" means to repeat the previous chord.

Abide with Me

Words by Henry Francis Lyte; Music by William H. Monk

TEMPO: Moderate   RHYTHM: None   COLOR: Organ

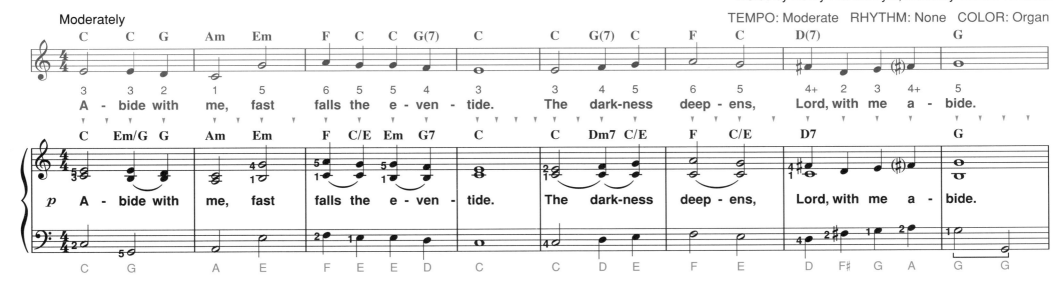

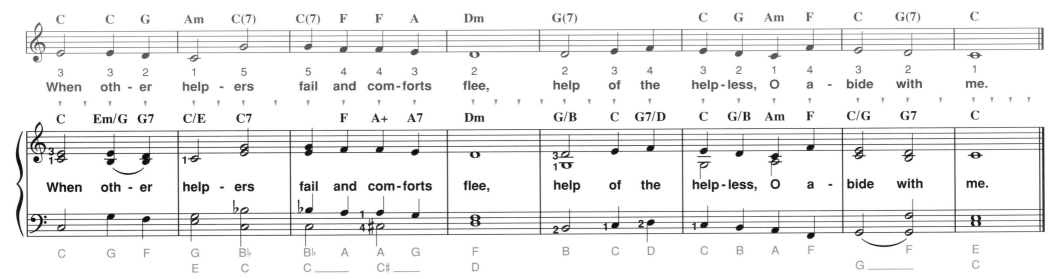

Additional Verses

2. Swift to its close ebbs out life's little day,
Earth's joys grow dim, its glories pass away.
Change and decay in all around I see,
O Thou who changest not, abide with me.

3. I need Thy presence ev'ry passing hour;
What but Thy grace can foil the tempter's pow'r?
Who like Thyself my guide and stay can be?
Thro' cloud and sunshine, O abide with me.

4. Hold Thou Thy cross before my closing eyes,
Shine thro' the gloom, and point me to the skies.
Heav'n's morning breaks, and earth's vain shadows flee,
In life, in death, O Lord, abide with me.

In the Sweet By and By

Words by Sanford F. Bennett; Music by J.P. Webster

TEMPO: Moderate   RHYTHM: None*   COLOR: (Reed) Organ

206   *Play chords where their symbols appears. A "/" means to repeat the preceding chord.

Additional Verses

2. We shall sing on that beautiful shore
   The melodious songs of the blest,
   And our spirits shall sorrow no more,
   Not a sigh for the blessing of rest.
   (Repeat Chorus)

3. To our bountiful Father above
   We will offer our tribute of praise
   For the glorious gift of His Love
   And the blessings that hallow our days.
   (Repeat Chorus)

IT IS WELL WITH MY SOUL

Words by Horatio G. Spafford;
Music by Phillip P. Bliss

TEMPO: Moderate   RHYTHM: None*   COLOR: Organ

208

*Play each chord where its symbol appears. A "/" means to repeat the preceding chord.

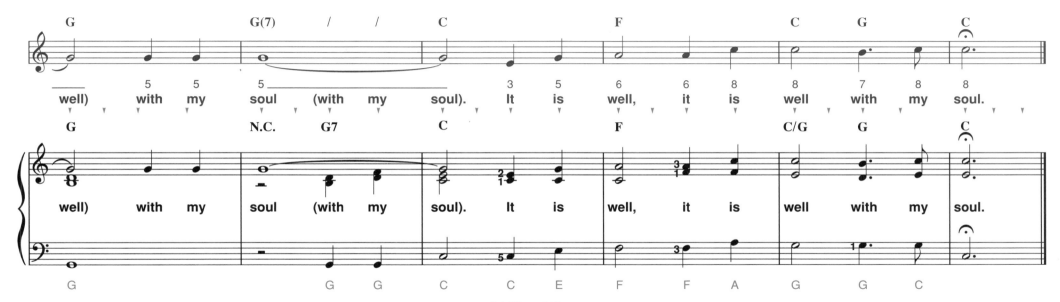

well) with my soul (with my soul). It is well, it is well with my soul.

well) with my soul (with my soul). It is well, it is well with my soul.

Additional Verses

2. Though Satan should buffet, tho' trials should come,
   Let this blest assurance control,
   That Christ has regarded my helpless estate,
   And hath shed His own blood for my soul.
   (Repeat Chorus)

3. My sin — oh, the bliss of this glorious thought —
   My sin — not in part, but the whole,
   Is nailed to the cross and I bear it no more,
   Praise the Lord, praise the Lord, O my soul!
   (Repeat Chorus)

4. And Lord, haste the day when the faith shall be sight,
   The clouds be rolled back as a scroll,
   The trump shall resound and the Lord shall descend,
   "Even so" — it is well with my soul.
   (Repeat Chorus)

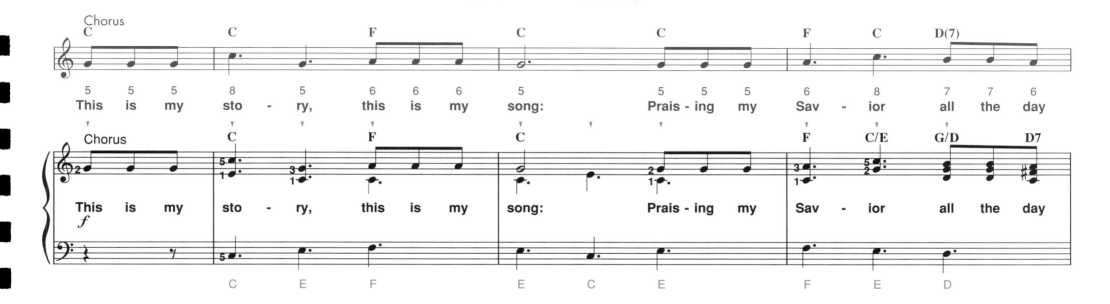

Additional Verses

2. Perfect submission, perfect delight,
   Visions of rapture now burst on my sight.
   Angels descending bring from above
   Echoes of mercy, whispers of love.
   (Repeat Chorus)

3. Perfect submission, all is at rest,
   I in my Savior am happy and blest.
   Watching and waiting, looking above,
   Filled with His goodness, lost in His love.
   (Repeat Chorus)

Beautiful Isle of Somewhere

Words by Jessie B. Pounds;
Music by John S. Fearis

TEMPO: Moderate   RHYTHM: None   COLOR: Organ or Reed Organ

Land of the true where we live a - new, beau - ti - ful isle ___ of some - where!

Land of the true where we live a - new, beau - ti - ful isle ___ of some - where!

Additional Verses

2. Somewhere the day is longer,
   Somewhere the task is done;
   Somewhere the heart is stronger,
   Somewhere the guerdon won.
   (Repeat Chorus)

3. Somewhere the load is lifted,
   Close by an open gate;
   Somewhere the clouds are rifted,
   Somewhere the angels wait.
   (Repeat Chorus)

Beyond the Sunset

Words by Virgil P. Brock; Music by Blanche Kerr Brock

TEMPO: Slow   RHYTHM: None   COLOR: Flute, Harp, Celeste or Vibraphone

Additional Verses

2. Beyond the sunset no clouds will gather,
   No storms will threaten, no fears annoy;
   O day of gladness, O day unended,
   Beyond the sunset, eternal joy.

3. Beyond the sunset a hand will guide me
   To God, the Father, whom I adore;
   His glorious presence, His words of welcome,
   Will be my portion on that fair shore.

4. Beyond the sunset, O glad reunion,
   With our dear loved ones who've gone before;
   In that fair homeland we'll know no parting,
   Beyond the sunset, forevermore.

214

America (My Country 'Tis of Thee) (page 224)

While still a student at theological seminary in 1831, Samuel Francis Smith was asked by the renowned church composer Lowell Mason to write words for several German melodies. The German air he chose first, he later found, was not really German in origin but rather the setting for the British anthem, "God Save the King," which had first appeared anonymously about 1745. Smith's lyrics were premiered at the 1831 Fourth of July celebration of the Boston Sunday School Union, conducted by Mason. It is interesting to note that American patriots of the Revolution, who knew the tune even if Mason and Smith did not, had already sung political lyrics to it, among them "God Bless George Washington" and "God Save the Thirteen States." After completing his theological degree, Smith went on to become a prominent Baptist minister, teacher of modern languages and editor of *The Christian Review*. He died in 1895.

America the Beautiful (page 216)

Katherine Lee Bates, an English teacher at Wellesley College, was on vacation in the Rockies in 1893. She had ridden a creaky vehicle much like a prairie wagon most of the way up Pikes Peak and hiked the rest. Still, she was unprepared for the magnificent view awaiting her at the top—beautiful beyond words, mountains stretching russet and violet as far as the eye could see under a vast sky of azure that embraced a carpet of golden fields and green valleys. Impulsively she jotted down the line "O beautiful for spacious skies," and later she expanded it into a set of verses, including a reference to the "alabaster cities" that she had seen at the World Exposition in Chicago on the same trip. The poem was published in the *Congregationalist* magazine two years later and became immediately popular. Numerous musicians suggested that they would be honored to write settings for it, but Bates instead selected the tune "Materna," composed in 1882 for the hymn "O Mother Dear, Jerusalem" by New Jersey organist-choirmaster Samuel A. Ward, which she felt best conveyed the majesty and true spirit of her verses.

Give Me Your Tired, Your Poor (page 218)

As early as 1865 a French historian proposed the gift of a statue to the United States as a symbol of French and American cooperation in the American Revolution and a commemoration of the country's Centenary in 1876. French sculptor Frédéric Auguste Bartholdi created the plans for the copper colossus, originally called "Liberty Enlightening the World," which was shipped to New York and assembled in 1887—with a sonnet by Emma Lazarus from her *The New Colossus* inscribed upon its base—causing immediate excitement worldwide. When, in 1949, Irving Berlin sought a magnificent finale for his musical *Miss Liberty*, based on the drama surrounding the statue's fund-raising and completion, he selected Lazarus's words. "Nobody's ever thought of using those lines in a song," he told his friend Gordon Jenkins, "and I can tell you it's going to stop people cold." Perhaps he responded with special sensitivity to her verses because he himself had been a Russian immigrant who had found hospitality and fame in this new, welcoming country. While the Broadway show was not a success, several of its songs, among them "Give Me Your Tired, Your Poor," continue to lead vivid lives of their own.

God Bless America (page 220)

Irving Berlin came to America in 1893, when his parents left Russia to escape persecution. As a World War I draftee in 1918, he was assigned to create songs for an Army show, *Yip! Yip! Yaphank*. (Yaphank, on New York's Long Island, was the site of an Army camp.) "God Bless America" was composed for that show, but Berlin, afraid of being thought a flag-waving superpatriot, cut it. The song was shelved until Kate Smith sang it on her radio program for Armistice Day, 1938, when it met with immediate and lasting success. Berlin said later, "I've tried to express my feelings in this song, which is not just a song but an expression of my gratitude to the country that inspired it." True to his decision not to profit financially from the piece, he diverted all its immense royalties and other income to the Boy Scouts and Girl Scouts of America. When Berlin celebrated his 80th birthday in 1968 on the *Ed Sullivan* television show, he chose to perform "God Bless America." Arguably the greatest American songwriter, Irving Berlin passed "beyond the sunset" in 1989 at the ripe old age of 101.

The Star-Spangled Banner (page 222)

On the morning of September 13, 1814, when the War of 1812 with England had been going on for nearly two years, attorney Francis Scott Key boarded a British warship in Chesapeake Bay under a flag of truce in order to secure the release of his friend William Beanes, who had been arrested as a prisoner. That night the English bombardment of Fort McHenry in Baltimore Harbor started. As dawn began to break, Key and Beanes scanned the outline of the fort through the smoke of battle to see which flag flew over it. So deep were his emotions that Key wrote a four-stanza poem describing the events. Within days, it was published as a broadside (a large folio sheet) titled "The Defence of Fort McHenry," along with mention of the well-known English drinking song "To Anacreon in Heaven," to which it was to be sung. Baltimore newspapers reprinted the poem, and the sheet music quickly appeared under the more euphonious title "The Star-Spangled Banner." The melody of "To Anacreon in Heaven," composed by John Stafford Smith in about 1775, had had some 80 different printed lyrics associated with it in America by the early 19th century—most of a patriotic nature. The Congress of the United States declared "The Star-Spangled Banner" the official national anthem on March 3, 1931.

AMERICA THE BEAUTIFUL

Words by Katherine Lee Bates;
Music by Samuel A. Ward

Moderately slow and stately

TEMPO: Moderately slow   RHYTHM: None*   COLOR: Organ

*Play each chord where its symbol appears. A "/" means to repeat the previous chord.

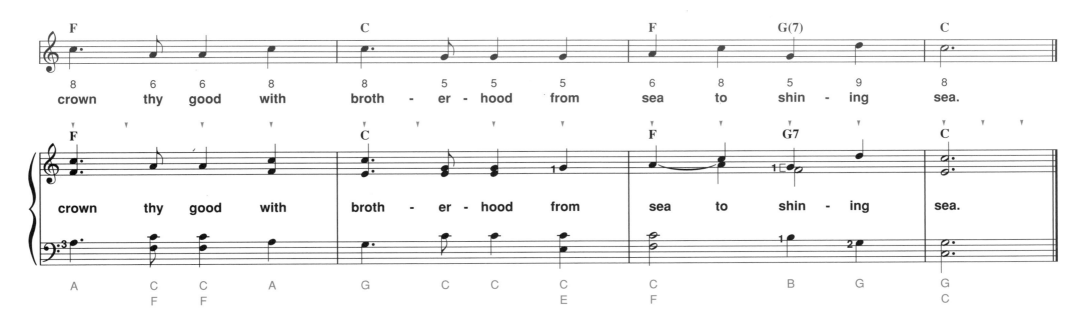

crown   thy   good   with   broth - er - hood   from   sea   to   shin - ing   sea.

Additional Verses

2. O beautiful for Pilgrim feet,
   Whose stern impassioned stress,
   A thoroughfare for freedom beat
   Across the wilderness.
   America! America! God mend thy ev'ry flaw,
   Confirm thy soul in self-control,
   Thy liberty in law.

3. O beautiful for heroes proved
   In liberating strife
   Who more than self their country loved
   And mercy more than life!
   America! America! May God thy gold refine,
   Till all success be nobleness
   And every gain divine!

4. O beautiful for patriot dream
   That sees beyond the years,
   Thine alabaster cities gleam
   Undimmed by human tears.
   America! America! God shed His grace on thee,
   And crown thy good with brotherhood
   From sea to shining sea.

Give Me Your Tired, Your Poor

Words by Emma Lazarus;
Music by Irving Berlin

TEMPO: Moderate   RHYTHM: None   COLOR: Strings, Vox Humana or Harp

218

GOD BLESS AMERICA

Words and Music by Irving Berlin

Rather fast in 4, or broadly in 2, with each ♩ receiving one beat

TEMPO: Rather slow   RHYTHM: March   COLOR: Brass Ensemble, Synth. Reed or Strings

God bless A-mer-i-ca, land that I love,

God bless A-mer-i-ca, land that I love,

stand be-side her and guide her thru the night with a light from a-

stand be-side her and guide her thru the night with a light from a-

bove. From the moun-tains to the prai-ries to the o-ceans

bove. From the moun-tains to the prai-ries to the o-ceans

pp   *gradually getting louder*

220

Words by Francis Scott Key;
Music by John Stafford Smith

TEMPO: Moderately slow   RHYTHM: None*   COLOR: Brass Ensemble

*Play each chord where its symbol appears. A "/" means to repeat the previous chord.

Words by Samuel
Francis Smith;
Music Traditional

*Play each chord where its symbol appears.